Kickback

A remarkable new law reveals how you get
what you want by putting others first

Robert Urbanowski

Library and Archives Canada Cataloguing in Publication Data

Urbanowski, Robert, 1967 –

Kickback: a remarkable new law reveals how you get what you want by putting others first /
Robert Urbanowski.

ISBN 978-0-9810370-0-4

1. Helping behavior. 2. Altruism - Psychological aspects.
3. Self-actualization (Psychology). I. Title.

BF637.H4U73 2008
158.1   C2008-903867-3

Printed in Canada
2008/1

Robert Urbanowski
Calgary, AB
W: www.lawofcontribution.com
E: info@lawofcontribution.com

ATTENTION ORGANIZATIONS:

Discounts available on multiple-copy purchases of this book for educational purpose or fund raising. For pricing information contact our Business Development Department at:

T: 403-689-7774
E: info@lawofcontribution.com

Contents

What Is the *Law of Contribution*?

The Effects of the *Law of Contribution* on Your Life

Why We Don't Contribute—The Two Great Lies

How to Benefit from the *Law of Contribution*

Introduction
More than a Good Idea!

This book unveils the discovery of a remarkable new law that reveals the original formula for prosperity, greatness and fulfillment. Although this law has not been previously defined, it has been active in your life since the day you were born, regulating your level of success, fulfillment and happiness. When you cooperate with this law, you feel your best and experience your finest moments. When you violate this law (even unknowingly), you feel your worst and those violations have ultimately contributed to your failures.

Virtually all lasting success and happiness require adherence to this law—in your personal life, your career, or even your business. Even though the definition of this law has not been understood until now, most people innately feel it deep within themselves. Most truly successful people have followed this innate guiding principle in their life. This book will unveil the dynamics of this law, and before you finish reading, you will agree that this law has been an essential part of both the successes and failures in your life.

I must warn you, however, that your initial instinct may be one of skepticism. The reason that this law has not been discovered until now is that the principle is counterintuitive. At first glance, it doesn't seem like it could possibly work. As an example, one of the first editors to read a copy of this manuscript put it this way: "At first I wasn't sure that I agreed with what you were saying. But by the time I was done with the book, I felt that

I had been on a journey. This book changed me." Most people who read this book admit to a similar experience where their uncertainty turns to enlightenment.

What is this newly discovered, powerful, yet remarkably simple law? It is called the *Law of Contribution*. The *Law of Contribution* is founded on the premise that you get more in life by focusing outward, on others, rather than by focusing inward, on yourself. This law demonstrates that all actions produce a kickback that is favorable when you focus outward on others' needs and a kickback that is destructive when your focus on self is overextended. Where virtually all self-help programs encourage centering your thoughts on yourself, your goals, your needs and your desires, the *Law of Contribution* demonstrates that such a focus could actually create barriers to obtaining those things. The paradox is that, in order to achieve a life of abundance, we must work to *first* meet others' needs rather than our own.

This fresh, new approach to true success tends to run contrary to commonly accepted opinion. That's because the real power of the law is hidden from us due to years of cultural conditioning. It has become a societal norm to focus on our own satisfaction, not on the needs of others. It's a generational way of life. We are the *me* generation. Something is happening that is causing us to turn inward, to focus more and more on ourselves. Everything around us is conditioning us to ask of ourselves, "How can I get what I want?" and "How fast can I get it?" The idea that contributing to others is a foundational basis for success and fulfillment conflicts with what we are conditioned to believe. Yet this is precisely why this message is so relevant and necessary for us today.

The essence of our generational way of life is that we focus on ourselves, our needs and our desires and, for the most part, ignore the needs of others. There is a problem with this default mode of operation. When we follow the common wisdom or prevailing cultural norms, most of us do not achieve the level of success or fulfillment we desire. Why? Perhaps we are violating one of the greatest and most significant laws of life—the *Law of Contribution*—without even realizing it. Much of what we are conditioned to believe and do actually works against us. Our inward-focused lifestyle prevents us from realizing a higher level of success and fulfillment, and makes it increasingly difficult to get what we want in life—whether at home, at work or in business.

The *Law of Contribution* provides timely insight into a concept that, once understood, is refreshingly simple and practical, yet obviously powerful. It contains the power to change, motivate and help us live more abundant and fulfilling lives. Its simplicity means anyone can understand and work with it in his or her life, regardless of age, income or IQ. Its power means everyone can reap the benefits of understanding how to harness the power of this law.

An understanding of the *Law of Contribution* is essential for the greatest achievements in business and in life. When you understand and begin to apply the *Law of Contribution* it will bring you greater success as you define it—whether personal fulfillment, improved relationships, career advancement or even a deeper grasp of the meaning of your life.

Think of the *Law of Contribution* as a lever that makes it possible for you to accomplish what would otherwise be very difficult. A lever works to help raise or lift something by reducing the amount of force required to do so. The *Law of Contribution* works the same way. It enables you to use what you have now—your abilities, gifts, talents and personality—as a lever to create more benefits for yourself, your company or your family.

Surprisingly, it's not by focusing on what you want; rather, it's by focusing on the needs of others and by contributing what you have to offer that creates the greatest leverage for you.

The *Law of Contribution* is not just a "good idea." It's a law that is active in your life, whether you want it to be or not. It is a law that produces a predictable result—a kickback—that is favorable when your actions cooperate with the law, but unfavorable when your actions violate the law. Since this is the case, wouldn't it be to your advantage to understand the dynamics of a law that so powerfully impacts your life? What if you could gain some insight into the forces that predict the very quality of your life?

In the pages that follow, you will learn what makes this law work, and you will also find many stories and examples that bring the practical power of this law to life. This book is designed to be an easy read. It's simple. Yet its message is powerful enough to make a significant impact on both your life and the lives of those around you. By the time you finish this book, you may even agree that if there was ever a single idea that could contribute to a different and better world, this just may be it.

Chapter 1
A Generational Problem

As you sit here reading this book, *where* and *who* you are is the sum total of your own choices. You chose your profession. You chose your spouse, your friends and, in a sense, your neighbors. Some of your choices were made consciously and others were made unconsciously. Some choices were *proactive* and others were *reactive*. Nonetheless, *you* chose how your life has turned out. Or did you?

Although we live in a society where we have the right to choose our own destinies, the simple truth of the matter is that our decisions are heavily influenced by others. We like to think that we are directing our own paths. Yet our choices might be less our own than we recognize. Instead, many of our choices are made based on what scientists call "social proof," but what I will refer to as *social guidance*.

In many ways, our generation—the *me* generation—evolved into what we are today because of the power of social guidance. What is social guidance? It is a psychological mechanism by which human beings look to others to guide their own actions—a fancy name for peer pressure. In short, we tend to view a behavior as more correct to the degree that we see others performing it. We assume that, when a lot of people are doing something, it must be the right thing to do. When we see a group of people gathered in a park, we tend to walk over and join them. We like to like things that others like, whether clothes, cars or activities. We know this is true; it's what makes actions and items popular.

Social guidance often happens on an unconscious emotional level. We don't consciously say, "All these people are wearing red jeans. I'd better get some too!" Nevertheless, we eventually find ourselves wearing them as well. Often, we simply can't help ourselves. It's hardwired into our brains. Using social guidance to validate our decisions is something that human beings have been doing throughout history.

Think about human beings in the Stone Age. They didn't possess many of the technological tools we take for granted today. If they came across a stream, they couldn't simply pull out a kit and test the water for parasites. Instead, they used social guidance to help them make decisions. If they saw other people drinking from the stream, they would assume the water was safe to drink. Likewise, if they wanted to know where to find the fish in the stream, they couldn't just turn on the fish finder in their canoes. Instead, they would paddle along until they found a spot where other fishers were gathered and join them. In this way, and many other ways, they used social guidance for their very survival.

Strikingly, modern people aren't much different. Despite our advanced technology, we are still heavily influenced by social guidance. If we are trying to decide which movie to see on a Friday night, we're likely to read a review or choose a movie that someone else has suggested is worth watching. Likewise, in deciding which products to purchase, most people choose one of the top two brands in that product category. This is a proven fact. We buy what's most popular, which is a reflection of what others are buying.

Of course, it can make sense to learn from the experiences of others. However, there are times in which the reliance on social guidance leads to nonsensical results. For example, in an experiment called the Asch Line Test, psychologist Solomon Asch demonstrated how other people could affect our decision-making. In his study, Asch told participants that they were going to participate in a line study to test "perceptual judgment." Asch showed a diagram with bars like those in the figure below to college students in groups of eight to ten. He told them he was studying visual perception and that their task was to decide which bar on the right was the same length as the one on the left. As you can see, the task is simple, and the correct answer is obvious. Bar "A" on the right is clearly the same length as the bar on the left.

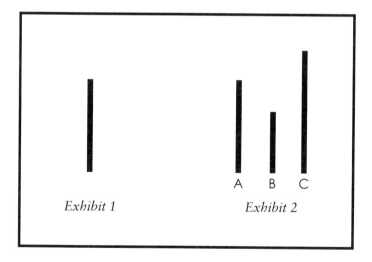

Exhibit 1   *Exhibit 2*

Asch staged the test. Only one of the students in each group was a real subject. All the others were confederates who had been instructed to give incorrect answers on certain trials. He asked the students to give their answers aloud and arranged for the real subject to be the next-to-last person in each group to announce her answer so that she would hear most of the incorrect responses before giving her own. Would she go along with the crowd?

To Asch's surprise, 74 percent of participants who were set-up to hear false answers conformed to the majority at least once. When faced with a unanimous wrong answer by the other group members, most people made the decision to agree and give an obviously incorrect response in order to remain comfortable within the group. Asch was disturbed by these results: "The tendency to conformity in our society is so strong that reasonably intelligent and well-meaning young people are willing to call white, black. This is a matter of concern."[1]

Of course, you may be thinking young people are particularly susceptible to peer pressure. Besides, what's the harm in giving a wrong answer in a silly study? Well, I assure you that people of all ages make decisions based on social guidance, even when the stakes are significant.

A fascinating example of social proof has been dubbed the "Werther effect," so named after the lead character in Goethe's novel *The Sorrows of Young Werther*. In his research, David Phillips demonstrated that the suicide rate increases dramatically in those areas where a suicide story has been highly publicized. Phillips found that within two months of every front-page suicide story, an average of 58 more people than usual kill themselves. In a gruesome illustration of the principle of social guidance, an uncomfortably large number of people decide suicide is an appropriate action for them because someone else has done it.[2]

In his book *Influence: The Psychology of Persuasion*, Robert Cialdini explains the power of social guidance at work in adults, describing a phenomenon called *pluralistic ignorance*. Pluralistic ignorance occurs when people look to others for clues to appropriate behavior, yet those others have no more insight or knowledge than themselves. It's the classic example of the blind leading the blind, and the results are often predictably tragic. The results were particularly tragic in 1964 for Catherine Genovese, who was stabbed to death over a period of 35 minutes while 38 neighbors looked on. None of these witnesses telephoned the police until after the woman was dead and silent.

Initially, the media characterized the inaction of her neighbors as cold and uncaring, the result of urban alienation and apathy. However, later research by Latané and Darley revealed that no one had helped precisely because there were so many observers. Each witness looked to the other witnesses to determine what to do. Since no one else was acting, they interpreted the situation as a non-emergency. In other words, they were in a state of pluralistic ignorance.

This hypothesis was supported in subsequent research by Latané and Darley. They determined that people were less likely to receive help as the number of bystanders increased: "...a New York college student who appeared to be having an epileptic seizure received help 85 percent of the time when there was a single bystander present, but only 31 percent of the time with five bystanders present."[3] In other words, the more people who stood around and did nothing to help, the greater the likelihood others would do the same thing.

As you can see, pluralistic ignorance can lead otherwise caring and compassionate people to act just the opposite. Even worse, sometimes in our effort to follow the leader, we end up just like the hunted American buffalo. There are two features of buffalo that make them especially susceptible to erroneous social guidance. First, their eyes are set in their heads so that it is easier for them to see to the sides than to the front. Second, when they run together in a stampede, it is with their heads down and low, so they cannot see above the herd. As a result, Native American hunters realized that it was possible to kill tremendous numbers of buffalo by simply starting the herd running toward a cliff. The animals, responding to the thundering social guidance around them, did the rest, running toward and over the cliff to their deaths.

Today, marketers use a similar strategy to get consumers running headlong into trouble by purchasing and consuming an excess of products that are not in their best interests. The marketing of tobacco products is a perfect example of using social guidance to drive the herd to its ultimate demise. For years, cigarette manufacturers marketed smoking as "cool" (or should I say, Kool?) Despite ample evidence of the harmful effects of smoking, these companies were able to stampede millions of people into literally killing themselves one puff at a time as they attempted to run with the "in crowd."

One of the most recent lies promoted through advertising can be seen in credit card commercials. These commercials often promote credit as giving you "freedom." You can get away from it all or buy whatever you want. However, the truth is that credit card companies sell *debt*. A debt is an *obligation*—the exact opposite of freedom. How do they do this? They pay famous people to stand in front of a camera and tell you that this is "their" credit card. They show you pictures of people having fun on vacation and doing whatever they want, all because they have this certain credit card. The credit card companies are appealing to your natural response to social guidance. If others use that card and get those results, then you could and should too.

I could cite example after example of how marketers use social guidance to affect our behavior. Yet this is not a book about social guidance. This is a book about decisions. So why all the hoopla about social guidance? Because we are being increasingly conditioned to make decisions that are driving us over a cliff. We are being sold a lifestyle that is unhealthy for us—a lifestyle that promises to give us everything we need and want, but is doing the exact opposite.

In a very real sense, we are quickly becoming like John Henry Fabré's now famous processionary caterpillars. Fabré, the great French naturalist, conducted an experiment with a group of processionary caterpillars, so named because these caterpillars blindly follow the one in front of them. Fabré filled a flowerpot with dirt and then carefully arranged the caterpillars in a circle around the rim, so that the lead caterpillar actually touched the last one, making a complete circle. In the center of the flowerpot, he placed some pine needles, which is food for the processionary caterpillar.

Sure enough, the caterpillars began marching around the circular flowerpot in a procession. Around and around they went for seven days and nights, at which point they dropped dead from exhaustion and starvation. Despite the fact that they were literally inches away from their life source, they failed to see it because they were so busy following the caterpillar in front of them.

Much of our society has become just like these processionary caterpillars. We fail to find nourishment and fulfillment because we are so focused on following the caterpillar in front of us, who, in turn, is following the caterpillar in front of him. Sadly, those around us are not acting on the basis of superior information, but are reacting to the social guidance around them. As a result, we all just keep marching round and round, never getting any closer to the things we *really* need in life. This is despite the fact that what we need is easily within our grasp and ready for the taking.

In short, we are being misled. Society presents the idea that having more, pursuing pleasures such as a bigger house, a nicer car, another vacation, a certain achievement and a better appearance are the things that bring fulfillment—to others and to us. But do these things really work? Who could we ask to find out? How about the very people that our society upholds as having it all? Why don't we ask the people who have all of these things whether they bring fulfillment? Let's ask the people with money, fame, beauty, sex appeal and achievement if these things really work.

What does Brad Pitt say about success and personal gain? In an interview with *Rolling Stone* magazine, he said,

> *The emphasis now is on success and personal gain. I'm sitting in it, and I'm telling you, that's not it. I'm the guy who's got everything. I know. But I'm telling you, once you've got everything, then you're just left with yourself. I've said it before and I'll say it again: it doesn't help you sleep any better, and you don't wake up any better because of it.[4]*

Think about it. Brad Pitt has more fame and fortune than any ten people could ever dream of having. He is widely recognized as one of the best-looking men in Hollywood and is currently with a woman every bit as attractive as he is. He has everything Madison Avenue tries to sell us. Yet even he is left wondering, "Is this all there is to life?" And Brad Pitt is not alone. Time and again, people who have grabbed the brass ring and achieved everything that is supposed to make them happy, have come away empty-handed.

Take, for instance, Tom Landry, the legendary coach of the Dallas Cowboys. In 1960, Landry became the first head coach of the expanded Dallas Cowboys. In his first full season as their head coach, the Cowboys completed a perfect season—a perfectly horrible season, that is. They finished with a record of 0–11–1. The team performed only slightly better over the next four years. It wasn't until Landry's seventh season with the Cowboys that they had their first winning season.

However, Landry's persistence finally paid off after 12 years, when his team won the Super Bowl in 1972. You would think that, after struggling more than a decade to achieve every coach's dream, Landry would have been as fulfilled as any man could be, right? Well, here is what the great coach had to say about his triumph: "The overwhelming emotion—in a few days, among the players on the Dallas Cowboys football team—was how empty that goal was. There must be something more."[5]

Landry is not the only Super Bowl champion to express this sentiment. John Burrough, retired NFL star, reflected on his 1998 Super Bowl win by saying, "In the middle of all the explosion and hoopla and hype, all I could think was, '*Is this it? It this all it is?*'"[6] Perhaps Tom Brady, the quarterback of the New England Patriots, said it best. After winning his third

Super Bowl at the age of just 28, Brady had the following conversation with *60 Minutes* interviewer Steve Kroft.

> **Brady:** Why do I have three Super Bowl rings and still think there's something greater out there for me? I mean, maybe a lot of people would say, *"Hey, man, this is what it is. I reached my goal, my dream, my life."* Me, I think, *"God, it's got to be more than this."* I mean this isn't, and can't be, what it's all cracked up to be.
>
> **Kroft:** What's the answer?
>
> **Brady:** I wish I knew…. I wish I knew.[7]

Now, you may ask, "What about beauty? Does that work?" After all, it is the subject about which philosophers and poets have waxed eloquently. Men have fought and died over the love of a beautiful woman. Surely, the attainment of beauty is worth the effort. Perhaps. But I think that one of the most beautiful women in Hollywood would disagree. Here is what Halle Berry has to say on the subject of physical beauty:

> *Beauty? Let me tell you something, being thought of as "a beautiful woman" has spared me nothing in life, no heartaches, no trouble. Love has been difficult. Beauty is essentially meaningless, and it is always transitory. I can't believe what people do to themselves [to make themselves look beautiful], the excess, and then they end up distorted. Worse, they still have that hole in their soul that led them to change themselves to begin with.*[8]

It doesn't matter what people obtain or achieve; "success" never shines as brightly as they are told it will. We see fame, fortune, beauty and accomplishment and think we want them, but the people who have them tell us there is more to life. So why, then, do we so desperately desire that which will not provide fulfillment or lasting happiness? Because we've been conditioned by social guidance to want it. After all, everyone else wants it, and is pursuing it, so the evidence tells us that it must be worth pursuing. Like the processionary caterpillar and the American buffalo, we blindly follow what we see others doing without regard for the consequences.

And trust me, there are consequences. In fact, our society is living evidence that things have gone terribly wrong. While every objective indicator of well-being in Western society is increasing, every *subjective* indicator of well-being is decreasing. We have more purchasing power, higher education levels, daily advances in medical science, and even greater access to music and entertainment than ever before. We are a society of "superstars" who have it all. Yet look at what is happening to us.

Depression is doubling every 20 years, and it strikes at a much younger age. According to a Harvard Medical Center study, the rate of childhood depression is increasing by an astounding 23 percent per year.[9] In fact, preschoolers are now the fastest-growing market for antidepressants.[10] Depression is projected to be the second largest killer after heart disease by 2020.[11] Correspondingly, suicide rates are increasing in the same way. Among young people aged 10 to 14 years, suicides have doubled in the last two decades.[12] Worldwide, suicide now ranks among the top three leading causes of death among those aged 15 to 44 years.[13] In the USA, one suicide occurs every 16 minutes. For every few pages of this book you read, another person will have taken his or her life.

The divorce rate has steadily risen over the last 40 years. In that time, the fastest-growing marital status category was "divorced persons." The number of divorced adults has quadrupled since 1970.[14] While the United States has traditionally had the world's highest divorce rate, the rate of divorce in other countries is exploding. The number of annual divorces in Japan more than doubled in the ten years from 1990 to 2000.[15] The divorce rate in China has increased five-fold since 1979![16] Likewise, divorces in Switzerland were up 40 percent from 1990 to 1998 alone.[17] In Canada, the number of men getting more than one divorce more than tripled from 1973 to 2003.[18]

The prevalence of overweight and obese Americans has increased dramatically for both adults and children. Among adults aged 20 to 74 years, the prevalence of obesity more than doubled, increasing from 15 percent (1976–1980 NHANES survey) to 32.9 percent (2003–2004 NHANES survey). The two surveys also show that the prevalence of overweight young people tripled in virtually all children and teenage categories. It is estimated that today 66.3 percent of Americans age 20 years and older are overweight or obese.[19]

To make matters worse, stress is on the rise. Stress is believed to trigger 70 percent of visits to doctors and 85 percent of serious illnesses. These numbers seem to be verified by a 2004 American Psychological Society survey reporting that two-thirds of Americans say they are likely to seek help for stress.[20] Stress is also deemed a major factor in the two leading causes of death—cancer and heart disease. And stress figures prominently in many other diseases.

Perhaps the greatest irony is occurring in our finances. Although as a society we are wealthier than ever, our personal finances are a bigger mess than ever. Bankruptcy filings in the USA increased almost ten-fold, from about 300,000 in 1980 to more than 2 million in 2005. Bankruptcies rose 30 percent in 2005 alone. Household debt as a percentage of household disposable income is at a record high, following the same trend as personal bankruptcies.[21]

Here we clearly see the paradox wrought by our reliance upon social guidance to make decisions for our lives. We've come to the point where the attainment of society's fantasy is becoming the individual's nightmare. Our blind pursuit of money, sex, fame and accomplishment is literally driving us over a cliff.

Interestingly, Cialdini warned of the danger of social guidance in his book, *Influence*. He also suggested there comes a time when we may need to apply the emergency brake to avoid running headlong over the cliff. He says, "We need to check the machine from time to time to be sure it hasn't worked itself out of sync with the other sources of evidence...." In other words, we need to look around and do a "reality check."

Unlike the American buffalo, we don't have to run with our heads down toward impending disaster. We can stop and look up. We can re-examine the way we've been approaching life. We can ask the question: "Is our desire to have it all preventing us from having the life we innately crave?" Perhaps it's time for all of us to stop long enough to examine some factual evidence, rather than listening to what's being promoted around us.

Chapter 2
A Timely and Relevant Solution

In the previous chapter, I spelled out the problem—that our inward-focused lives are providing everything but true fulfillment. But why? How can having it all lead to desolation and despair? Believe it or not, the answer is because we are going about life with exactly the *opposite* approach we are meant to. We are asking the wrong questions and, as a result, coming up with the wrong answers.

> *We accept many notions because they seem to be the logical answers to our questions. But have we asked the right questions?*
>
> - Harold L. Klawans, M.D.

Everything around us is teaching us to ask just one question—"How can *I* get what *I* want?" We are truly living in a *me* society. We have been conditioned by social guidance to ask, "What's in it for me?" In fact, this question has become such a mantra that you see it printed on T-shirts, bumper stickers and billboards. The message is simple: it's all about you. You can be happy and fulfilled as long as you get the most "stuff"—the biggest house, the nicest car, the most attractive mate, the corner office, you name it.

Think about it. Isn't that the one constant of every commercial you see on television—it's all about you? Burger King says, "You can have it *your* way." McDonald's agrees, "*You* deserve a break today." And why do you deserve a break today? As L'Oreal will tell you, "Because *I'm* worth it."

You can tell the ideals of a nation by its advertisements.

- Norman Douglas

Now, you may be thinking, "What's wrong with that? After all, I am the customer. Shouldn't companies cater to *my* needs?" The answer is "yes." Yet the truth is that advertisers are not catering to our true needs. They are catering to what we *think* we need—what we've been conditioned to believe we need. In truth, they are catering to the needs they've helped create in us by continually getting us to ask the wrong question: "What's in it for me?"

There is an old saying that goes like this, "If they can get you to ask the wrong question, they don't have to worry about giving you the right answer." Well, marketers have us asking the wrong questions: "How can I make more money? How can I get a larger home? How can I get a fancier car? How can I look better, feel better and smell better? How can I? How can I?"

The problem with these questions is that they are inward focused. They create an overextended focus on yourself. Many of the problems we experience stem from an incorrect focus. We focus inward when we should focus outward. Rather than focusing inward and asking, "What's in it for me?" we should be focused outward and asking, "How can I give?" and "What can I contribute?"

Life's most persistent and urgent question is: What are you doing for others?

- Martin Luther King, Jr.

In this book, I will introduce you to a simple principle that I have termed the *Law of Contribution*. This law is based on a simple premise—*you were designed for contribution*. As you will see, our very human design requires that we *contribute* in order to be happy and fulfilled, in order to succeed, and even in order to be healthy—emotionally, mentally and physically. In addition, the things we want most in life require that we contribute to the needs of others. In short, the more we focus on contributing in life, the more we receive and the closer we get to a fulfilling life.

The *Law of Contribution* is just as real as the law of gravity or any other natural law, and it works in the same fashion. A natural law exists before its discovery and acceptance by the scientific community. For instance, the law of gravity existed well before that apple fell on Sir Isaac Newton's head and it would still exist, even if we were completely ignorant of it. In the same way, the *Law of Contribution* has been operating in your life whether you know it or not. Your current level of fulfillment and happiness is directly tied to your adherence to the *Law of Contribution*. There are no exceptions. To the extent that you've violated the *Law of Contribution*, you've experienced pain and loss and, to the extent that you've adhered to the law, you've experienced joy and abundance. It's just that simple.

> *It is impossible for us to break the law. We can only break ourselves against the law.*
>
> - Cecil B. DeMille

Interestingly, some people follow the *Law of Contribution* without any conscious knowledge of it. As a result, they seem to just naturally draw to them all of the good things in life, although they probably couldn't tell you why. Just as with the law of gravity, these fortunate few just seem to "stumble" upon the *Law of Contribution*. However, the rest of us are not so lucky. We need to be shown the way. Fortunately, this law can be learned and used to create the results we *really* want out of life.

After all, the discovery of a natural law is nothing but the discovery of cause and effect. Someone observes that if x occurs, then y follows. Once we learn this cause and effect, we use the knowledge to cope with the world around us. And we can use our knowledge not only to survive, but also to thrive. For instance, over the centuries, we've learned enough about rivers not only to avoid being swept away in them, but also to harness their power to create electricity. In this same manner, we can learn to observe the *Law of Contribution* and harness its power to create the abundance of mental, physical, spiritual and social riches that we are all so desperately seeking.

The *Law of Contribution* is just that powerful. Yet it requires a major shift in thinking. It requires that you abandon many of the beliefs that you've learned from society and accept a new truth—that contribution is the key to success and happiness—not the attainment of selfish wants and desires. By positing that you get more by giving more, the *Law of Contribution* is counter-intuitive. It's certainly counter to the "It's All About Me" outlook in our society. In fact, it probably qualifies as outright heresy.

Interestingly, airplane travel was once considered heresy. In 1870, the Methodist churches of Indiana were having their annual conference on a college campus. The college president addressed the attendees and told them about all of the exciting inventions coming their way in the coming years. Among these inventions was a contraption to allow humans to fly like birds.

After this presentation, Bishop Wright took the podium to condemn the college president's remarks as heresy. He explained that the Bible reserved flight for the angels. Upon returning home from the conference, the bishop told his family about these "ridiculous" comments. However, 32 years later, these comments didn't seem quite so ridiculous when the bishop's two sons, Orville and Wilbur, made their historic flight at Kitty Hawk.

Why were the sons able to do what seemed impossible to their father? Because they were willing to look beyond the so-called "truths" of the day to observe the real law in effect—in this case, the law of aerodynamics. Well, you can achieve the same results if you're willing to look behind the "truths" of the Me Generation.

> *It's always wise to raise questions about the most obvious and simple assumptions.*
>
> - C. West Churchman

In short, I'm asking you to do what the American buffalo cannot do—stop and look around. When we stop long enough to look at the *real* evidence, we find that the people who really have it together—the people who have abundance in *all* aspects of life—are focused on giving and contributing—not simply on getting what they want for themselves. Sure, in the process, they end up reaping great rewards for themselves, but it's important not to confuse cause and effect. They have *because* they contribute—not the other way around.

We cannot live only for ourselves. A thousand fibers connect us with our fellow-men; and along those fibers, as sympathetic threads, our actions run as causes, and they come back to us as effects.

- Herman Melville

Many people in our society have done just that—confused cause and effect. They see the end result and think, "Hey, I want that too. If I can have what they have, then I too will have a life of fulfillment and joy." Yet what they fail to see is the commitment these people have shown to a common principle of contribution. It's adherence to the *Law of Contribution* that causes all of the outward signs of prosperity and not the other way around.

Of course, this is just the opposite of the message conveyed through our media. For example, I recently saw an advertisement for a heated belt that causes the wearer to sweat. According to the manufacturer, if you wear this belt for a little while every day, you will magically lose pounds and inches without any physical effort. This is a classic example of confusing cause and effect.

Sweat isn't what causes weight loss—it's physical exertion that makes you sweat. Sweat is just a by-product (effect) of calorie-burning activity. The real catalyst of weight loss is, of course, exercise. Yet the manufacturer of this product was attempting to sell the effect without the cause.

Sadly, this is a common strategy with marketers. If they can't produce the cause, they'll sell you the effect. As intelligent consumers, it's time to stop buying into this nonsense. It obviously isn't working for us. Even a child could tell us that.

In fact, I recently encountered a young adult who did just that—my nephew Mark.

During a family gathering, this "guy" walked into the room. At first, I didn't recognize him. It turned out that he was Mark. Now, how did I not recognize my own nephew? Because he had lost 160 lbs since the last time I had seen him. He literally looked like a different person.

I asked him how he did it. He told me that he finally learned enough about nutrition to know what really works when it comes to weight loss and physical health. Obviously, he didn't go out and get a Ph.D. in nutrition. He simply learned a few simple *truths* that told him that he wasn't going to lose weight with magic powders, potions or contraptions. By making a few simple decisions (and sticking to them), he was able to transform his physical body—and the possibilities for his entire life.

Knowledge of the *Law of Contribution* can be just as powerful for you with just one caveat—*you must make it a guiding principle in your life*. What is a guiding principle? It's a value or truth you use to filter your decisions. For many people, the guiding principle is, "What can I get out of this?" This is the guiding principle that has been thrust upon us for as long as we can remember. We've been told to choose our careers, our friends, our neighbors and even our churches on this basis.

Yet the *Law of Contribution* teaches us just the opposite. The question is not, "What can I get out of it?" Instead, it is, "What can I put into it?" How can I make an impact in my community, my nation and the world? This is the guiding principle of life's most successful people, and if the *Law of Contribution* is going to have any power in your life, it must become your guiding principle as well.

You can chant positive affirmations until your throat is sore or you can do twelve-step programs until you've worn down the heels of your shoes, but trust me, if you are focused on anything other than contribution, you will struggle to possess lasting success. And just like any other natural law, the *Law of Contribution* isn't a law of convenience. Gravity just doesn't work when you want it to work or when it's in your best interests to work. Gravity works *all* of the time. It's the law.

The same principle holds true for the *Law of Contribution*. Sure, you can have an "it's all about me" attitude and get *some* of what you want (fame, fortune, etc.), but you will never get all of what you *need* (fulfillment, contentment, joy, etc.). Contribution is the operating system on which all your personal and business programs must run. It is the foundation on which all achievement must be built. It's the filter through which all decisions must be made. It's the framework on which all personal and business relationships must grow.

Without it, we end up like much of our society—getting what we *think* we want, but still missing what we need and crave most.

And with that thought in mind, in the next chapter we're going to answer the question, "What *is it* that we need and crave most?" It is by answering this question that we are better able to understand exactly how this counterintuitive *Law of Contribution* actually works.

Chapter 3
What's Really Driving Us?

What is it you think you really want in life? If you're reading this book, it's because you're looking for something. You're looking for a better way to motivate your employees, you're seeking meaning in life, you want more intimacy in your marriage, you hope for more success or financial abundance, or maybe you simply enjoy learning about new concepts and ideas that help make your life better. Whatever it may be, you're reading this book for a reason... you want something. What do you want?

What Do You *Really* Want?

The simple truth is that although there are things you want, everything you do and pursue is really driven by the desire to satisfy four basic human needs. Why is it important to know what these needs are? These needs regulate your level of satisfaction in life (is that a good enough reason?). It's actually not the "things" you want, it's the end result you think they will bring. The end result you crave is actually the fulfillment of four innate needs: the need for physical sustenance, security, significance and love.

These needs are genetically hardwired. They cannot be changed. Every human is born with and motivated by these same desires. What makes individuals unique is that we each have preferences for how we'd like our needs met. For example, if you and I were to sit down in a restaurant for lunch, you might order a healthy salad and I might order a fat-saturated hamburger—those are our individual preferences. But neither of us can change the fact that we need food to survive. We can't deposit quarters into a slot in our shoulder, we can't connect an electrical cord to an outlet in the back of our head and we can't pour gasoline into a tank in our feet. The only form of energy that can fuel a human being is food. Our innate needs are part of our DNA.

The Four Innate Needs

So while each of us might answer the question, "What do you really want in life?" differently, we are all really pursuing the same end result—satisfaction of the same four needs. Although it might be hard to believe, your spouse, your teenage kids and your boss all have the same desires as you do—only expressed in such a way that you might never guess it to be true.

We all live with the objective of being happy; our lives are all different and yet the same.

- Anne Frank

There are three important benefits to understanding what these needs are. First, rather than following social guidance when making decisions about what we want, we can stop to consider what it is we are *really* trying to accomplish. What needs are we really trying to satisfy?

Second, understanding these needs sheds important insight into the actions of those around you. This is especially important when striving to understand those you love—your spouse, your children, your family or friends.

Third, if you are going to benefit from the *Law of Contribution*, which requires that you contribute to the needs of others, it is critical that you understand others' needs. What are their real needs and how can you help them have a better life?

Here is a brief overview of these needs and exactly how they regulate our behaviors in life.

The Need for Physical Sustenance

The first most basic human need is the need for physical sustenance. This is the need to provide the basic necessities of life—food, water and air. Without any one of these things, we would not live long. Humans die in a matter of minutes without air, in a matter of days without water and in a matter of weeks without food. Although we might take the satisfaction of this need for granted, 24,000 people on this planet die from the effects of hunger each day. On average, about 34 people will die from hunger in the time it takes you to read this page. Food, water and air are not optional luxuries. They are needs.

The Need for Security

Security is our innate need to defend and protect what we value most—beginning with our very lives. All humans are hardwired to defend themselves and to seek out security for themselves and those they love. The need for security is embedded deep within our DNA and is exactly what we need to protect ourselves from a real physical threat, such as a wild animal or a burglar invading our home. Because we have this intrinsic design, we don't have to think twice in order to defend ourselves from danger. The human body is equipped with a nervous system that automatically tells it to fight or flee in these situations.

This "fight-or-flight" response is an automatic, inborn survival mechanism that prepares the body for action. When you sense a threat of any kind, an inner trigger begins pumping out stress hormones such as adrenaline, which get the heart racing, send the blood pressure soaring, put muscles on alert and help prepare you for outrunning a saber-toothed tiger, a landslide or your mother-in-law. This physiological response in your body provides you with instantaneous energy and mental alertness to enable your defense and survival. Not a bad design.

Feeling physically secure, however, does not quench the innate need for security. Although the root of this need stems from our requirement to defend our physical bodies, we respond in the same manner any time we perceive that something we value is threatened. Our need for security demands that we defend and protect *whatever* we value, which includes our loved ones and things like our finances, our jobs, our reputations, and so on.

Any time something we value is threatened, our bodies go into high alert. We instinctively begin to feel uneasy, scared or fearful. Our emotions are activated along with the fight-or-flight survival response. It's a natural response designed to make us aware of potential risk. For example, you might feel fear or anxiety when you learn of a terrorist attack in your country, when your job is threatened or when your retirement assets are suddenly devalued, say, in a stock market crash. You'll feel the same fear of loss if your business is suffering, your spouse has been unfaithful to you or you learn that someone you love has cancer. In fact, these things don't actually have to happen. Very often, just the *possibility* of loss is enough to trigger the feelings of fear, stress and anxiety. For this reason, we crave security in all of its forms—physical, emotional and financial.

The Need for Significance

John Dewey, one of America's most profound philosophers, said, "The deepest urge in human nature is the desire to be important." This is the desire for *significance*—to feel important, valuable and of consequence in the world. We desperately want to know that we matter and that our lives are necessary. By design, every person is made with the need to feel capable of contribution—capable of having something to offer.

The craving for significance serves a healthy purpose in our lives and is necessary for our development as human beings. We have been imbued with this innate need for significance that won't be satisfied until we become all that we are capable of becoming and contribute what we are capable of contributing.

> *Our prayers are answered not when we are given what we ask, but when we are challenged to be what we can be.*
>
> - Morris Adler

It is the desire for significance that enables great discoveries and contributions. Civilization would not have advanced to this point without men and women who were driven to achieve. Throughout history, the need for significance has driven people to build pyramids and monuments in their honor. This same need has also driven people to engage in activities that matter: founding universities and hospitals; finding cures for diseases; and inventing things like the airplane, the automobile, electricity, the computer, the telephone and much of what has shaped our world today. Our sense of value is affirmed when we contribute to life in this way. We matter. We feel valued and important.

Man's search for meaning is the primary motivation in his life.

- Viktor Frankl

Hasn't this been the case for you ever since childhood? In school, the teacher asked a question and you knew the answer. How did you feel? You were excited, right? Your little hand shot up and waved wildly, while you practically screeched, "I know! I know! Pick me!" And when you answered the question correctly, how did you feel? You felt important. You felt strong. You felt good about yourself. Right?

The same is true in your adult life. Sure, the questions are more complex, but you're still just as excited when you know the answer to, say, increasing sales in your department, curing a sick patient, resolving a customer complaint, reducing delivery times or what have you. We all enjoy being recognized as being a person of ability.

This is why athletes spend their entire careers in pursuit of a title: a Super Bowl ring, an Olympic gold medal or anything that confirms they are the best. It explains why businesspeople spend their lives at work, without their children and family, in the name of achieving whatever objective they seek—money, position or praise.

The desire for significance explains why people amass fortunes they will never spend, or own homes too large for their requirements, or drive expensive cars, or wear the latest fashions. It is the innate need for significance that drives us all in this way.

The Need for Love

Love is a genetically wired need to feel valued. We feel valued when we are accepted, admired, cherished and appreciated by others.

Consider how you would feel if the people in your life—at home, at school or at work—made you feel valued in this way (accepted, admired, cherished and appreciated). What if they validated your worth, appreciated you, approved of you, cared for you and cherished and encouraged you? What if you received more reassurance, understanding and acceptance? Think about that for a minute. How would that make you feel? Wonderful, right? It would not only affect your happiness, but your confidence, effectiveness and ability to achieve. Love is a strong motivating factor in your life.

The supreme happiness of life is the conviction that we are loved; loved for ourselves, or rather, loved in spite of ourselves.

- Victor Hugo

Experiencing this kind of love is necessary not only for our happiness, but also for our emotional and physical health—even our survival.

From the day you were born, you needed love for your survival almost as much as food, water and air. The now famous 1945 study by René Spitz confirmed this to be true. The study occurred in a hospital where a group of children—all under three years of age—were fed and clothed adequately, but because of too few nurses, they were given very little personal care or attention. No one talked to them, carried them around, or cuddled them. The results were devastating. Within two years, one-third of the children had died and the rest had severe intellectual disabilities. The evidence is clear. Love isn't just desirable for children—it's *essential* to their proper mental and physical development.

Children need to receive love and confirmation that they are valued in order to develop emotionally and mentally—and to survive. The need for love is equally essential throughout our adult life. Science confirms that love is responsible for more than our happiness and harmony; it is necessary for our survival.

In 1965, Dr. Berkman, at the California Department of Health Services, conducted a study to determine the link between love and our physical well-being. Dr. Berkman and her colleagues examined almost 7,000 men and women living in Alameda County, California. The study found that those who did not have social and community ties—such as contact with friends or relatives, a spouse, or social groups—were 1.9 to 3.1 times more likely to die during the nine-year follow-up period. The researchers continued to follow the mortality rate of these people for an additional eight years. They found the same results: those with the strongest social ties had dramatically lower rates of disease and premature death than those who felt isolated and alone.[22]

Many other studies support the same findings, like a similar study conducted in Sweden. More than 17,000 men and women were followed for a period of six years. The individuals that were the most lonely and isolated were almost four times more likely to die prematurely during this period.[23]

The main fact of life for me is love or its absence. Whether life is worth living depends on whether there is love in life.

- R. D. Laing

The absence of love does not just affect our physical well-being—without love, we suffer emotionally and the quality of our lives is reduced. People who live without love, live with emotional pain.

A freelance reporter from the *New York Times* once interviewed Marilyn Monroe. She was aware of Marilyn's past and the fact that, during her early years, Marilyn had been shuffled from one foster home to another. The reporter asked, "Did you ever feel loved by any of the foster families with whom you lived?" "Once," Marilyn replied, "when I was about seven or eight. The woman I was living with was putting on makeup, and I was watching her. She was in a happy mood, so she reached over and patted my cheeks with her rouge puff. For that moment, I felt loved by her."[24]

Imagine that! She only felt loved once during her entire childhood. Is it any wonder that, despite all her outward success as an adult, she never recovered from that deficit of love? Her death by drug overdose is consistent with what many people resort to without love.

In many cases, the suffering that comes from a life without love is more than people can stand. Like Marilyn Monroe, people who don't feel loved often don't want to live. Studies show that people who are alone and isolated are the predominant victims of suicide. Pioneer French sociologist Émile Durkheim con-

cluded in a milestone 1897 study of suicide that "the critical factor in determining suicide was the degree of social cohesion."[25]
He also found that unmarried men and women were more likely
to commit suicide than those who are married. Without others
in our life to care for us, life has little meaning. The pain becomes so great that, for some people, ending their own life becomes their tragic solution.

> *Love… has the greatest power, and is the source of all our
> happiness and harmony….*
>
> - Plato

Without love, our behaviors become destructive. Psychologist, author and scientist Havelock Ellis said, "When love is sup-
pressed, hate takes its place." When people don't feel valued,
when they feel lonely and isolated, they become angry, which
shows in their behavior. They will often turn to whatever measure is easiest in order to ease the pain: drugs, alcohol, excessive
work, excessive television watching, and so on. Their behavior is an attempt to ease or erase the pain caused by the absence of love.

Clearly, love is more than a nice feeling. Love is a genetically
wired, human *need* that we cannot live without. When we are
loved (i.e., when we feel valued), we are happy, healthy and fulfilled—without it, we suffer.

Lower-level Needs versus Higher-level Needs

To summarize, the four basic human needs include the following:

Need	Description	Level
4. Love	Desire to be valued and cared for by others	higher-level needs
3. Significance	Desire to feel important, worthy and necessary	*Fulfillment Needs*
2. Security	Desire for safety. To protect what we value	lower-level needs
1. Physical Sustenance	Desire for physical sustenance: food, water, air	*Survival Needs*

You will notice these four needs are divided into two important categories: (1) lower-level needs and (2) higher-level needs. The lower-level needs can be described as *survival needs*. The desires for physical sustenance and security ensure our survival and are common to all living beings. Animals function purely on this level. They focus all of their attention and efforts on obtaining food and water and protecting themselves from the elements and predators. The wildebeest doesn't lie awake at night thinking, "Am I fulfilled? Am I content? Is this all there is?" For the wildebeest and all other animals, the only question is, "Am I still alive?" If the answer is "yes," all is right with their world.

For better or worse, human beings are more complex. In addition to our survival needs, we also have *fulfillment* needs. These are the higher-level needs that make us unique from all other creatures on the planet. Only human beings have the ability to experience the states of love and significance. We feel best in life when these needs are satisfied. Conversely, our lowest moments occur when these needs are unmet. If you're currently unhappy in life, it's likely because one of your higher-level needs is not being met.

An Excellent Design

The four basic human needs guide human existence and are critical to our quality of life. These needs drive our behavior. Our minds constantly regulate the status of these needs and set off alarms to drive us to seek sources to fulfill them. Without these internal alarms, we would be in big trouble. For example, if the need for food were not wired into your alarm system, you wouldn't instinctively get hungry or thirsty. You could starve to death simply by forgetting to eat. At the very least, you would run the risk of illness from not eating as regularly as you should.

Similarly, without the need for security, your body would not automatically prepare you for fight-or-flight in the face of danger. As a result, you would be more prone to death or serious injury due to accident or attack, because you simply wouldn't be able to move quickly enough to evade the danger or take adequate precautions to avoid it altogether.

Imagine a life without the need for significance. Without the innate need to feel valued and important, who would take the initiative and run the risk of doing great things? Who would climb a mountain, set sail for distant lands or work on a cure for AIDS? In short, the human race would have no driving force for achievement.

In the same way, life would be unbearable without the innate craving to feel love. In fact, without the need for love, we couldn't even live together in society. Because we want to be liked and accepted, we treat people with a basic level of respect and kindness. Imagine a person without the need for love—the person who doesn't care what others think of him, or whether or not they accept him. At best, such a person would be indifferent to the people around him. At worst, this person would wreak havoc on others. In fact, we have a name for such people: "sociopaths." In the past, a single Jack the Ripper, Jeffrey Dahmer or Charles Manson has been able to terrorize an entire city. Imagine what our world would be like with a society full of these people.

As you can see, our needs serve healthy purposes. Without the need for food, we would starve. Without the need for security, we would fail to defend. Without the need for significance, we would do nothing. Without the need for love, we would destroy one another. Our needs make our existence possible and our lives worth living.

Three Key Observations

Three key observations about these four innate needs help bring the *Law of Contribution* into clear focus.

1. You are happiest when your needs are met.

We are only truly satisfied and happy in life when our innate human needs are met. Of course, for most of us living in the Western world, lower-level needs are largely met. Few of us have ever faced any real danger of starvation or homelessness. Therefore, for those of us who were lucky enough to be born on this part of the planet, our greatest struggle for satisfaction has been meeting our higher-level needs—the needs of significance and love.

To illustrate my point, I ask you to take a moment to think back over your life and answer the following questions:

At what points in your life have you felt the very best?

_____

_____

What was happening in your life to make you feel this way?

_____

_____

Your answers likely fell into one of two categories:

1. You felt significant (i.e., you achieved something).

2. You felt loved (e.g., valued, cherished, appreciated).

Perhaps your best times in life were when your marriage was working well and you felt close and intimate with your partner. Or they may have been when you spent time with close friends or family, such as during the holidays. Or maybe you experienced highs in your life when you won an award or accomplished a difficult goal, like losing weight, completing a marathon, being selected for a team at school or earning a promotion at work. Or perhaps it was something else altogether. Yet it certainly fits into the categories of significance and love. You felt your best when your higher-level needs were met.

The opposite is true as well. Once again, to allow me to illustrate, please answer the following two questions:

At what points in your life have you felt the very worst?

_____

_____

What was happening in your life to make you feel this way?

_____

_____

Your answers likely fell into one of two categories:

1. You experienced a loss of significance (e.g., failure, loss of acclaim, a hit to your reputation, a sense of helplessness).

2. You experienced a loss of love (e.g., a death, divorce, the end of a valued relationship).

Perhaps your lowest point in life is marked by a divorce (your parents' or your own). Perhaps it was related to the death of a loved one. Or maybe your worst times involved a failure of some kind—the loss of a job, a business failure, or financial bankruptcy. Or, once again, it may have been something else altogether. However, in all likelihood, your lowest moments were related to your innate needs for love and significance being unmet.

2. You'll do whatever it takes to have your needs met.

Because there is considerable pain tied to unfulfilled needs, you will do *whatever it takes* to meet your needs. Of course, this is obviously true in regards to our lower-level needs. If someone held your head underwater, you would do *whatever* it took to get to the surface. Even if you are normally the type of person who wouldn't hurt a fly, you would kick, scratch, bite and claw at the other person until he or she let you go. Why? Because you *need* air and you will do anything to get that need met.

Well, it may surprise you to know that you are no less desperate to meet your higher-level needs. You will not let anything get in your way of meeting your needs for love and significance—even reality itself.

Some professionals believe people may even go insane in order to find the feelings of love and significance that they could not obtain in reality. For example, in his book *How to Win Friends and Influence People*, Dale Carnegie tells the story of a doctor treating one such patient.

> *I have a patient right now whose marriage proved to be a tragedy. She wanted love, sexual gratification, children and social prestige, but life blasted all her hopes. Her husband didn't love her. He even refused to eat with her and forced her to serve his meals in his room upstairs. She had no children, no social standing. She went insane—and, in her imagination, she divorced her husband and resumed her maiden name. She now believes she has married into English aristocracy, and she insists on being called Lady Smith.*
>
> *As for children, she imagines now that she has had a new child every night. Each time I call on her, she says, "Doctor, I had a baby last night."*

While most people do not go to this extent to meet their higher-level needs, many people do attempt to meet those needs in other unhealthy ways. For example, Sara, a 17 year old in Columbus, Ohio, got her need for significance met by starving herself. Suffering from anorexia, she recently entered treatment for her eating disorder. While in rehab, she admitted what drove her illness. "I guess I was attention-starved," she now says of her motivation. "I really liked being the girl that everyone looked up to, and the one they saw as their 'thinspiration.'" Fortunately, she finally came to her senses, admitting, "But then I realized I was helping girls kill themselves." She was getting her need to feel valued met in a very unhealthy way.

Once again, people will do *whatever it takes* to have their needs met. For some, that means pursuing achievement, fame, money or possessions as ways of establishing their worth to the world, even at the cost of their health and loving relationships with their families. Others assume enormous debts in order to possess a certain house, car, or clothing in an effort to increase their standing in the eyes of others.

3. *You are instinctively drawn to sources that meet your needs.*

The bottom line is that our needs for love and significance are so hardwired that we will pursue their fulfillment in even strange and unhealthy ways. We need them that badly. As a result, we are instinctively drawn toward things that fill our needs—even if unconsciously. Just as our brains force us to breathe all day without consciously thinking about it, our brains also unconsciously force us to seek love and significance.

We're just like birds that fly south for the winter. These birds don't necessarily *want* to fly several thousand miles. Nor do they discuss the decision with the rest of the flock and come to a reasoned conclusion that it would be best for the southern bird economy if they were to all vacation in Florida. Their need to avoid the cold weather of the northern climate drives them to fly south. Likewise, our need for love and significance drives us to get married, have children, pursue promotions and achievements, write books and engage in a host of other activities.

As a corollary, we instinctively return to previous sources of fulfillment. We're very much like the swallows at San Juan Capistrano. Year after year, they return to the same place. They never think, "Hey, maybe we should head down to Baja this year. I hear that the bugs are really tasty down there." They've found a place that meets their needs—San Juan Capistrano— and they will continue to return there each year until it no longer does. We are driven by similar instincts. When we find a person or place that meets our needs, we unconsciously find ourselves returning there again and again.

For example, if you find, say, a Chinese restaurant where the food is good and the staff treats you well, you will probably return to that restaurant whenever you feel like eating Chinese food. This will be the case even if your town has dozens of similar restaurants to choose from. Since you've found a restaurant that satisfies your need for Chinese food, you will most likely opt for the "sure thing."

In fact, the desire for the "sure thing" fuels our desire for committed relationships. Marriage is largely an effort to lock in a "sure thing." We've found a dependable source of love and therefore, we look to get a commitment to ensure that this source will *always* be available to us. We exhibit similar loyalty to our friends and employers if they are meeting our needs. We are drawn to reliable sources of need fulfillment, and we will devote considerable energy toward maintaining our relationships with these most reliable sources. That energy may be in the form of money or time or effort or love or *whatever it takes* to obtain our need fulfillment.

The Key to the *Law of Contribution*

Let's summarize the facts. We now know people feel their best when their needs are met; they will do whatever it takes to have their needs met; and they are naturally drawn toward sources that fill their needs. For this reason, whenever you *contribute* to another person's needs, whether as a person or a business, you naturally draw their energy toward yourself. Energy can be expressed with money, time, effort, love or whatever it takes to obtain the fulfillment of a need.

What people desire more than anything is a *secure* source of need fulfillment. Their actions are driven by this desire, and they gravitate toward sources of reliable fulfillment without even realizing it. Furthermore, they will offer their contribution of energy in whatever form necessary to fill their needs. The more you participate in the need fulfillment process by contributing, the more you draw energy—money, time, effort, love—to yourself or to your business.

As such, the *Law of Contribution* states, "*You get what you want when you give to meet others' needs.*" It's a lot like the old cliché, "You get what you give." Others have said, without realizing the significance of the statement, "If you help enough other people get what they want in life, you will eventually get what you want." However, the *Law of Contribution* is not an old cliché or tactic for manipulating others' behavior. It is a law with principles that must be obeyed if it is to work in your life.

This is the basis of the *Law of Contribution*. We all have needs that require input from others in order to be fully satisfied. Our programming is designed with a requirement for interdependence. Other people get their needs met when we contribute to them. We get our needs met as a natural response to our contribution. Contributing to one another is the trigger to obtaining the things we want and need most.

If people are so driven to have their needs met that some will even go insane to get them, imagine what you might achieve by understanding how to give people what they really want and need. That is what you will discover, beginning with the next chapter.

Chapter 4
Outward Focus: The Key to Need Fulfillment

We now understand why the *Law of Contribution* states, "*You get what you want when you give to meet others' needs.*" It's because people will do whatever it takes to have their needs met, and so, the more you participate in life by contributing to the needs of others, the greater your kickback—the more you receive in return. With this in mind, the next logical question is, "How do we meet others' needs?"

To maximize the effectiveness of this law in your life, you'll need to learn how to contribute to others in such a way that ensures you are actually meeting their innate needs. Otherwise, you'll end up frustrated and not understanding why the law doesn't work for you. Understanding exactly how to fill others' needs requires that you learn to become *outward focused.*

Outward focus is the ability to produce thoughts and actions that are centered on others, beyond yourself. To become outward focused, you'll need to understand how to identify the needs of others, and you'll need to know exactly what actions you can take to meet those needs.

Let's start with a basic explanation of how outward focus works. The diagram below illustrates the principle.

The inner circle labeled "Self" represents your life (or your business, organization, church, etc.). The outer circle represents

"Others," which includes other people in your life (your family, spouse, coworkers, friends, customers, shareholders, etc.).

Outward Focus

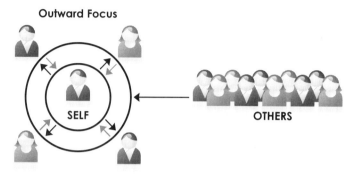

When you contribute in some way to others in your world (arrows pointing outward), you meet the needs of other people and, in doing so, you activate a response from the world—a kickback—(arrows pointing at you), where the people in your world begin flowing energy (money, time, love, etc.) back to you.

The more you give, the more you amplify the opportunity to receive even greater benefits in return. Let's have a closer look at what this means and how to apply it in the various arenas of our life.

What Is an Outward-focused Attitude?

Being outward focused starts with a willingness to help others: your employer, your employees, customers, spouse, children or even complete strangers—the poor, the elderly, the sick, and so on.

I think of love as looking outward. And so, our job, in order to serve God, or be more Godlike, is to focus on how much good you can do to others, and give very little thought to whether it's going to rebound to you. You can't keep it from rebounding to you.

- Sir John Templeton

The primary attitude driving outward-focused actions is a willingness to help others, even if they are not in a position to help you in return. Outward-focused people know that the universe responds to people who contribute to the common good. They don't buy into the scarcity mentality: that the pie is only so big, and that you must fight to get the biggest piece possible. They know that God has created an abundant world overflowing with blessings for everyone. As a result, they respond to life much like Christine Comaford Lynch.

> *I think that when people ask you for help…you should just jump in and help. Because there is nothing in it for you initially, but it sets in motion this energy that I cannot describe. When I was younger, I used to think, "I did such and such for Suzie-Q, so when I call her she should deliver." And then I realized how stupid that was, and that it doesn't work that way. When you help people out, other people, not necessarily the same people, will help you out. It just gets something rolling. Like when you are fortunate financially and you give money away. More money comes your way. There's some sort of "laws of the universe" that I think I'm starting to figure out.*

- Excerpt from *Good Business* by Mihály Csikszentmihályi

What Are the Seven Most Powerful (and Simple) Outward Expressions?

Understanding how to be outward focused is simple and easy. Think of it like the Golden Rule—treat others as you want to be treated. You want your needs met, and so do others.

The renowned speaker Cavett Roberts once said, "Three billion people on this planet go to bed every night hungry for food, but four billion people go to bed every night hungry for a sincere word of encouragement and praise." Roberts is right. The most widely unmet human need is the need to feel loved and significant. We want to feel valued and appreciated for what we do and who we are. Being outward focused means understanding this and being willing to offer outward expressions that validate the worth of other people in our life.

As an outward-focused person, you know that you may not be able to feed this need for everyone in the world, but you are willing to make an effort to feed as many people as possible in *your* world. Therefore, being an outward-focused person means being willing to offer simple outward expressions that meet the needs of those around you.

I have identified seven of the most common outward expressions. They are surprisingly simple to do, yet most rare and powerful.

Outward Expression #1: A Smile

The most basic outward expression is a smile. A smile is a universal expression that tells any person in any country that you are pleased when you see them. A smile expresses joy, affection and friendship. Everyone enjoys a smile because it is the most basic form of need fulfillment. The literal meaning of the word "smile" is "to look with favor or approval; to express cheerful acceptance." When you smile at someone, you immediately meet that person's needs for love and significance in the most basic way.

Can a simple smile really be so powerful? Yes! In fact, it is very likely that a smile has changed your entire life. If you're currently married or in a relationship, I can almost guarantee you that it all started with a smile. You and your eventual mate saw each other at a party, in line at Starbucks or wherever, and you smiled. That smile gave one of you the encouragement to approach the other and strike up a conversation. This conversation led to a date and then another and then another. It may have eventually led to marriage and children and a home and everything you hold dear in life—all because of a smile.

Well, if a smile can affect your entire life, then don't you think it can affect someone's *day*? Of course it can. Try injecting a smile when ordering your coffee at Starbucks, paying for your groceries, passing a coworker in the hallway, arriving home from work or even when talking to your mother-in-law. A smile can lift the spirits of another and even lift your own. And best of all, it requires so little investment of effort on your part, yet it offers a potentially great return.

> *A smile costs nothing, but gives much.*
> *It enriches those who receive,*
> *without making poorer those who give.*
> *It takes but a moment,*
> *but the memory of it sometimes lasts forever.*
> *None is so rich or mighty that he can get along without it,*
> *and none is so poor but that he can be made rich by it.*
> *A smile creates happiness in the home,*
> *fosters goodwill in business,*
> *and is the countersign of friendship.*
> *It brings rest to the weary,*
> *cheer to the discouraged,*
> *sunshine to the sad,*
> *and is nature's best antidote for trouble.*
> *Yet it cannot be bought, begged, borrowed or stolen,*

for it is something that is of no value to anyone
until it is given away.
Some people are too tired to give you a smile.
Give them one of yours,
as none needs a smile so much as he who has no more
to give.

The Value of a Smile
Rabbi Samson Raphael Hirsch

Outward Expression #2: Acknowledgement

How often do people receive acknowledgement or recognition? Not often. Think about it: when was the last time you sincerely acknowledged or recognized someone for something he or she did, or just because of who he or she is?

When you acknowledge other people, you affirm their value. It can be as simple as acknowledging their existence (e.g., "hello"), or acknowledging a skill (e.g., "You sing really well"), or acknowledging an accomplishment (e.g., "Good job on your presentation") or just acknowledging *anything* about them (e.g., "You have such a wonderful smile"). Everyone needs to be recognized as a person, and for what he or she has to offer. When you provide that acknowledgement, you lift the person's spirit and sense of value.

You can even change the entire course of someone's life with just a few words. This is exactly what happened to Nathaniel Hawthorne, who is widely acknowledged as one of the greatest American novelists of the nineteenth century. Yet Hawthorne didn't spend his early adulthood writing the works that would make him an icon in American literature. In fact, he did not publish his first collection of short stories until his early 30s. Instead, he worked for a customhouse in Boston.

In 1848, at the age of 44, Hawthorne lost his job and limped home to confess to his wife that he was a failure. Upon hearing the news that Hawthorne had lost his job and the family's sole source of income, Sophia Hawthorne exclaimed, "Now, you can write your book!" She then opened a drawer and pulled out a substantial amount of money. "I have always known that you were a man of genius. So every week out of the money you have given me for housekeeping, I have saved something: here is enough to last us for one whole year."

Just two years later, Hawthorne published one of the most revered works in American literature—*The Scarlet Letter*. The next year, he published *The House of the Seven Gables*. His writings earned him universal acclaim from the literary giants of his time. Herman Melville dedicated *Moby Dick* to Hawthorne "in appreciation for his genius." Edgar Allan Poe, who was generally critical of Hawthorne, wrote, "We look upon him as one of the few men of indisputable genius to whom our country has as yet given birth."

Yet all of these acknowledgments only followed the first words of acknowledgment from his wife on the fateful day in 1848. Her acknowledgement of Hawthorne's talent, and her encouragement to pursue a career as an author made all of the rest possible.

Outward Expression #3: Time Together

> *When we love something it is of value to us, and when something is of value to us we spend time with it, time enjoying it and time taking care of it.*

> - M. Scott Peck

Spending time with someone is another simple, yet powerful outward expression. Time is our most precious resource because it is irreplaceable. If you lose your home, your car or your money, you can get more, but you can never get more time. Once it has passed, it is gone forever. For that reason, when you spend your time with someone, you tell the person he or she is valuable. In the same way, your decision not to spend time with someone tells this person just the opposite. For instance, it's difficult for your spouse or children to believe you value them if you don't spend time with them. Spending time with people affirms to them that they are valued.

Outward Expression #4: Listening

The greatest compliment that was ever paid to me was when one asked me what I thought, and attended to my answer.

- Henry David Thoreau

When you listen to people—really listen to what they have to say—it affirms that you care about and value them. Of course, in order to listen, it means you have to stop talking. This is the hard part of listening—keeping *your* mouth closed. It is rare to find people who are willing to listen half as much as they talk. If you can do this when around other people, you become a rare and outward-focused person who naturally makes others feel valued. And the only thing you have to do is talk less and listen more. Make an effort to genuinely listen to what others have to say and notice what happens.

Outward Expression #5: Gratitude

When you show gratitude to people, it affirms their value—that what they did for you was important. There are a multitude of opportunities to do so every day. Our lives are interdependently linked to others—we rely on the help and services of other businesses and the people in those businesses every day. With each interaction, you have the opportunity to express a little bit of gratitude for the effort made by the person serving you. It doesn't require much. Looking the store clerk in the eye when saying "thank you" can demonstrate the sincerity of your gratitude. Simply saying with sincerity, "Thank you very much for your help" can be enough to validate the worth of the other person.

Think about this: if people go out of their way on your behalf, isn't an outward expression of gratitude the right response? Of course it is. We all know it is. Yet somehow it doesn't happen often enough. There is nothing more frustrating than doing something for someone who does not recognize our effort. We've all had the experience of helping an ungrateful person and walking away thinking, "Why did I even bother?"

When was the last time you offered gratitude to people in your life for the things they do for you? They need it. Just do it.

Outward Expression #6: Kindness

The little unremembered acts of kindness and love are the best parts of a person's life.

- William Wordsworth

Any kind gesture affirms the value of another person. It can be any act, great or small: sending flowers to a sick person, buying a thank-you gift, holding a door open, helping an elderly person load groceries, anonymously giving money to someone who needs it. Acts of kindness are simple to give, wonderful to receive and rewarding for both parties involved. Try offering a random act of kindness and notice how you feel.

Outward Expression #7: Respect

Respect has been defined as "the state of being regarded with honor or esteem. Willingness to show consideration or appreciation." There are many ways to show respect, but respect is really about placing value in another person.

Unfortunately, most people are selective about who they show respect for. They only show respect for people with impressive titles like judges, doctors and CEOs or people of noteworthy and famous achievements. Outward-focused people assume everyone is worthy of respect. They show the same regard for the gas station attendant as they do for the mayor of their town or its leading citizen.

These are just some of the simple ways you can express outward-focused actions to others in your life. As you can see, outward expressions are a form of the Golden Rule—treating other people as you want to be treated. By performing any of these outward expressions, you say to the other person, "You are important. You matter. You are worthy of my attention." In short, you are meeting their higher-level needs. You are treating people in the way we all want to be treated.

Every day, you have the opportunity to contribute outward expressions and meet the innate needs of *every* person with whom you come into contact. If you make a concerted effort to be outward focused in your interaction with others, I guarantee you will see a significant improvement in how you feel and how others respond to you. And as one of my friends once said to me, "I like guarantees."

What Are the Five Greatest Opportunities for Outward Focus in Life?

Five arenas in life give you the opportunity to be outward focused and reap the greatest rewards. These five arenas include your interactions with your children, your relationship with your spouse, your job as an employee, your role as a manager or leader, and your business activity. Let's look at each of these outward opportunities in more detail.

Outward Opportunity #1: With Your Children

Children benefit more than anyone by having their four basic needs met. When their needs are met when they are young, children gain a healthy foundation upon which they can build their lives. If you are a parent, your greatest and most significant opportunity for contribution is the one you have every day with your children.

The nature of a parent-child relationship provides ample opportunity for you to be outward focused. As the parent, you are meant to give without expecting anything in return. You put a roof over their heads, food in their bellies and clothes on their back. And what do your children owe you in return? Nothing. Sure, they may give you love, respect and adoration, but they aren't *obligated* to do so. All of the obligations in the parent-child relationship run one way—from parent to child. Being a parent is the ultimate training ground for living an outward-focused life.

As parents, we must focus on meeting our children's greatest need—the need for *unconditional love*. Children need to feel loved by their parents regardless of their behavior or achievements. They should not have to *earn* love by excelling in school or in sports. Regardless of their looks, grades, athletic prowess, awards or achievement, they should be safe in the knowledge that they are cared for and valued.

Your children's need for love and significance is every bit as strong as your own. If you don't meet these needs, they will look to other sources to do your job for you. These sources may come in the form of a bad crowd, a gang or even drugs. After all, each of these other sources guarantees a form of unconditional love and acceptance—even if it is an extremely destructive form.

So how do outward-focused parents meet their children's need for unconditional love? By giving it, of course. This means giving love and encouragement even when our children don't *deserve* it (remember, by the very nature of the relationship, they don't owe us *anything*). It also means not withholding love and affection just because they have failed or not performed to the level you hoped for or expected. In fact, during these times, they need a kind word or loving touch the most.

After all, when they succeed in school or sports, they will be surrounded by people affirming their worth. However, when they fail, their list of admirers will be short. As a parent, you should certainly be at the top of that list. When parents are outward focused with their children, they are likely to enjoy the relationship with their children, and raise children they can be proud of.

Outward Opportunity #2: With Your Spouse

A marriage (significant other) relationship can only work if both partners' needs are being met. Relationships only break down when the partners feel their needs are not recognized. Dr. Emerson Eggerichs, in his book *Love and Respect*, describes the basic needs of a husband and wife in a marriage. He explains that what a woman needs most from her husband is *unconditional love*, and what a man needs most from his wife is *respect* (a form of love).

Troubles begin in a marriage when the partners feel their needs are not being met. When a husband feels his need for respect is unmet, he has a natural tendency to react in a way that feels unloving to his wife. When the wife feels her need for love is unmet, she is likely to respond in a way that feels disrespectful to her husband. Without her need for love being met, she reacts without respect. Without his need for respect being met, he reacts without love. And so begins what Eggerichs calls the Crazy Cycle, whereby the actions of both husband and wife deprive each other of the need fulfillment they both require. When this happens and the needs of *both* partners go unmet, the relationship begins to break down.

Dr. John Gottman, a leading marriage researcher from the University of Washington in Seattle has done significant research that supports this premise. Gottman says that people enter into relationships for emotional fulfillment (need fulfillment). The relationship is a place where both people are, on a daily basis, requiring expressions from each other in order to have their needs met. Both parties bid for validation from their partners, desiring to receive some expression that affirms they are loved, respected and valued.

His research shows that husbands who eventually are divorced ignore the bid for validation from their wives 82 percent of the time compared to 19 percent for men in stable marriages. Women who later divorce ignore their husband's bids for validation 50 percent of the time, while those who remain married only disregard 14 percent of their husband's bids. The bottom line is that many relationships fail because people don't pay enough attention to the needs of the other.

You must be outward focused, and give to meet the needs of your partner, if you want your relationship to be fulfilling. People don't get married to have those relationships fail. However, most fail because people don't pay enough attention to the needs of the other person. Learning to be outward focused can help you enjoy your relationships in a healthy, new way.

Relationships are about "being in it together." In other words, *together* you must work toward meeting your respective needs. Relationships are about you *and* your partner, not you *or* your partner. After all, a marital relationship is meant to be the ultimate safe zone in which spouses can safely expect to have their needs met. When those needs are not met, bitterness can take root and the relationship can break down. At least half of marriages end in divorce.

When was the last time you provided encouragement to your spouse? When was the last time you showed gratitude for what he or she does for you? When was the last time you told your spouse how much you respect him or her? Being an outward-focused spouse means recognizing your spouse's needs and meeting them. Being an outward-focused spouse always means meeting your spouse's needs *first* without the expectation that your spouse will respond in kind.

Outward Opportunity #3: As an Employee

Being outward focused is not only the key to personal rela-tionships, but it is equally crucial in business relationships. Re-member, you get a job by demonstrating to your employer that you can meet her needs to have a particular task performed. You get promoted in that job by demonstrating that you can meet your employer's multiple needs. Obviously, being an outward-focused employee helps you in that effort. When you demon-strate to your employer that you are first and foremost interested in meeting the needs of the company, you become indispensable to the organization. In turn, the company is much more likely to meet your needs for financial compensation, approval, recogni-tion and so on.

Sadly, this won't always happen. However, you should try to remember that while your employer may sign your paychecks, you work for humanity. By that, I mean that you are rendering a service for your employer's customers, shareholders and the community-at-large. Therefore, if your employer is too self-ab-sorbed to recognize your contribution (and this does happen), you should still give your very best anyway because someone else will recognize your contribution.

Zig Ziglar tells a wonderful story about just such a situa-tion. In the story, he explains how he was a clerk working in a grocery store in Yazoo City. One day, he noticed that his coun-terpart at a competing store, Charlie, was performing his chores at an accelerated rate. Charlie was literally running from place to place as he performed errands. Zig says he asked his boss, "Why is Charlie doing all that running around?"

"Well, it appears to me that Charlie is looking for a raise. And I suspect he's going to get it too," replied the wise storeowner.

"How do you know that?"

"Well, because if Charlie's boss doesn't give it to him, I will."

And while this may be another one of Ziglar's extraordinary tales, it does contain a significant truth—the workplace responds to an outward-focused employee. You may not get your reward from your current employer, but if you make a concerted effort to meet its needs, *someone* will give you what you deserve.

In addition, you should try to keep in mind that your company is nothing more than a collection of human beings—all of whom have the four basic needs you have. Therefore, in your interactions with your coworkers and bosses, you should give the expressions of outward focus. In other words, you should remember to smile. You should show gratitude for your job and the opportunities it provides for you to contribute. You should acknowledge and recognize the achievements of your coworkers, bosses and the company itself. Remember, as humans, we are instinctively drawn to people who meet our needs and we will do *whatever it takes* to have those needs fulfilled. You become a magnet in the workplace when you are driven by the desire to contribute.

Outward Opportunity #4: As a Manager or Leader

The question of how to motivate employees has haunted businesses and managers for decades. Although there are many opinions and tactics for how to motivate workers, the bottom line is again quite simple. Employees are individuals with the same four core human needs every other person has. Like we discussed in chapter three of this book, those are the need for physical sustenance, security, significance and love. People come to work driven by their requirement to have those needs met. If you help them meet those needs, you will have employees committed to serving and contributing toward the needs of your organization. The theory for motivating people at work is simple—when employee needs are met, they will perform well and achieve. When their needs are not met, they will be frustrated and disengaged.

The great business management guru Douglas McGregor reflected on how employees view motivation: "Unless I perceive that you can somehow affect my ability to satisfy my needs, you cannot influence my behavior." In other words, employees respond best when you appeal to their innate needs. McGregor states that after a person's monetary needs are met, the most primary needs driving behavior are the needs for "respect, self-confidence, achievement, status, recognition and appreciation." Sound familiar?

The foremost principle in leadership is in complete sync with the *Law of Contribution*. That principle is that *leadership* is not *about you*. Real leadership is about understanding your responsibility to contribute to the needs of those you lead.

> *When you become a leader, success is all about growing others.*
>
> - Jack Welch

One of the largest studies undertaken by the Gallup Organization supports this thesis. The study surveyed over a million employees and 80,000 managers and was published in a book called *First Break All the Rules*. It came up with this surprising finding: If you're losing good people, look to their immediate supervisor. More than any other single reason, such supervisors are the reason people stay and thrive in an organization. And supervisors are the reason why people quit, taking their knowledge, experience and contacts with them—often, straight to the competition.

The book's authors, Marcus Buckingham and Curt Coffman, reflect on the requirement to meet employees' basic need for significance: "So much money has been thrown at the challenge of keeping good people—in the form of better pay, better perks and better training—when, in the end, turnover is mostly a manager issue." Beyond a certain point, employees' primary need has less to do with money, and more to do with how they're treated and *how valued they feel*. Managers who don't meet the needs of their employees, don't keep their employees. It's just that simple.

If you focus on monetary rewards to motivate employees, but fail to recognize their contributions, do not treat them fairly or do not demonstrate care for them as individuals, they will leave the moment someone offers them what they really want. They may even leave for less money if the opportunity to have their need for significance is met elsewhere. Obviously, in a time where good employees are hard to find and harder to keep, leaders should care about their employees' needs.

Interestingly, it may be even worse for a company when its employees stay under bad managers. Employees with unmet needs are angry employees. Since they can't resort to open hostility, they often resort to passive aggression. They dig in their heels and work slowly. They only do what they are told and no more. They omit giving the boss crucial information. In short, they make it more and more difficult for the company to achieve its objectives.

Great leaders know the secret. In his book *Good Business*, Mihály Csikszentmihályi explains, "Treating peers, customers and subordinates with respect is one of the most often repeated values endorsed by this group [great leaders]." As a manager and leader, unless you develop an outward focus and meet the needs of your employees, you are going to struggle endlessly to motivate them to do what you need done.

Outward Opportunity #5: Managing Your Business

Genuine care, concern and empathy for others and the desire to meet people's needs are not attitudes commonly associated with corporations. Corporations are often viewed as cold monsters, without soul or moral conscience. The only obligation of a corporation seems to be to make a profit—at any and all cost. The actions that corporations take in the name of fulfilling their obligation to make a profit are often ruthless, purely selfish and even immoral. Ironically, in the world of commerce, such actions are commonly accepted as a necessary function of business. If a company does not act to maximize its profits, shareholders will have its managers' heads!

With this in mind, does the *Law of Contribution* have any validity for a business, when its only motive seems to require it to be consumed with self, with its own need for profit? The truth is that a corporation, despite its flawed character, is not different from a person. A corporation can only get what it wants by focusing on meeting the needs of others first. Despite its need for profit, it must be outward focused if it is to survive.

Whose needs is the corporation required to meet? In order for a company to produce a profit it requires a customer, and it requires employees. As a result, a corporation cannot have its need for profit met without first focusing on meeting the needs of the people in its world—specifically, its customers and employees. The more a corporation meets the needs of its customers and employees, the greater chance it has to maximize its profit.

The great business guru Peter Drucker states accurately that the purpose of any business is nothing more than "to create a customer." Speaking about the purpose of a business, he states, "It demands that business define its goal as the satisfaction of customers' needs. It demands that the business base its reward on its contribution to the customer."[26] Unless a business has outward focus, it can't possibly accomplish its objective—the creation of a customer.

If the purpose of your business is to make a profit, rather than serve a need, imagine how that will affect your decisions. What does making a profit tell you about how to design and build your product (as cheaply as possible—who cares if it works)? What does it tell you about how to serve your customers (charge a lot, give a little)? What does it tell you about how to treat employees (pay little, demand much). A business must have an outward focus to recognize what its real objectives are—to serve a need.

When a business moves beyond its own internal politics and selfish needs, it can better understand what the customer really wants and needs. As a result, the business can put itself in a better position to receive the customer's repeat business. Remember, people instinctively return again and again to "sure thing" sources of need fulfillment. It should be the business of every business to be this source.

In the same way, a business requires employees to serve its customers and produce a profit. Without motivated and con- tributing workers, a company has little chance of satisfying its customers. Employees who work on behalf of the company have the ability to improve the company's bottom line. Clearly, the company needs its employees if it expects to achieve its goal and satisfy its shareholders.

In the same way that a person must be outward focused, a corporation must be outward focused if it expects to get what it wants in the end. The corporation's actions must purposefully meet the needs of those in its world.

In short, the key to being a great parent, having a loving re- lationship with your spouse, getting ahead in your job, enjoying an enthusiastic response from your team, or building a world- class business is outward focus. When you operate with a true outward focus, everything else just falls into place. By "true" outward focus, I mean an outward focus that is based on gen- uine care and concern for others.

The Care and Concern Factor

It's not enough to do things for others in the ways mentioned in this chapter. You must do so with an attitude of care and con- cern. When you do, you create a stronger bond with other peo- ple. Being outward focused means giving without expectation of anything in return, not giving *in order* to get. People can tell when you are insincere and they resent being manipulated. However, when you give with genuine care and concern for other people, the result is much different.

For example, if I provide for my family's needs but show little care or concern for them as individuals, I will be treated with the same level of disrespect. On the other hand, if I provide unconditional love in addition to food, money and shelter, I will get an abundance of love and respect in return.

In the same way, if I help customers with an "I'm just doing my job" attitude, I do not create a bond that causes the customers to return. On the other hand, if I help customers with an attitude of care and concern, I meet an additional need of the customers—their need for love. These are customers who will return to me time and time again.

If I contribute to my employer with a 9 to 5 attitude, I will get my 9 to 5 paycheck—and nothing more. However, if I contribute with an attitude of care and concern for the well-being of the organization, I am more likely to be compensated accordingly. My contribution will be repaid by my current employer—or by a future employer who will recognize my unique contribution. In the meantime, my talents and abilities are being enhanced to enable future contributions and rewards.

In many ways, the concept of outward focus is common sense. It's not that difficult to do, and it costs us very little. It's a kind of code of human conduct that we all agree should be followed. However, if this is the case, then why don't we all get the results we hope for? Why does this concept not seem to work for us? The reason is that we inadvertently create barriers that block the effectiveness of our efforts. In the next chapter, we'll discuss what it means to become inward focused, and how our unintentional doing so can produce destructive results in our life.

Chapter 5
Inward Focus:
The Barrier to Abundance

What Does It Mean to Be Inward Focused and How Does This Create Barriers to Getting What We Want in Life?

Inward focus is the propensity to focus on self more than on others. Essentially, it means to be *self*-focused. We are inward focused when we focus on ourselves, our needs and our desires, and we fail to recognize and contribute to the needs of others.

The problem with an inward focus is two-fold. First, by failing to recognize and contribute to the needs of others, you make it improbable that others will invest their time, energy, love or resources into you. Essentially, you create a barrier between yourself and others. Second, and ironically, the more focused you are on yourself, the less satisfying your life will be (I'll explain why in this chapter).

It's easy for us to become inward focused at times because *everything* we do is really driven by what we get from it. Even acts of kindness and altruism make us feel good, and those good feelings are what motivate our giving. In the same way, the premise of this book is that *you* will get something by learning to give to others. So while there is a natural tendency to be focused on self, being overly consumed with self works against us. This makes more sense when we understand how our inward focus is meant to serve us. The diagram below is a good starting point.

As you can see, the inner circle is *you* and the outer circle is the world in which you live. An inward focus is *necessary* to meet your lower-level needs—the need for physical sustenance and the need for security.

Need for Physical Sustenance

In order to meet your need for physical sustenance you must be inward focused. You *take* what you need for your *self* from the world—food, water, air—to survive. The resources you need to survive are not found within you. You must acquire and consume them.

Inward Focus

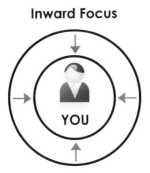

Need for Security

The need for security is the need to *defend* yourself. In protecting yourself from a threat, your focus must turn to your *self*-survival and protection. You have been hardwired with the fight-or-flight response, whereby your body instinctively produces adrenaline to empower you to run from or defend against attack.

Observations about Inward Focus

The following observations will help clarify the "position" we are in when inward focused.

1. The center of focus is *self*.

2. It is a *survival* response.
   This is how you are made to sustain your existence. In this state, you are concerned with your needs only to enable your survival. It's natural.

3. It is a *defensive* response.
   If you are being attacked, you will defend your-self—even if it means killing the attacker. In such a situation, you are not concerned about the other person. Your natural survival instinct causes you to defend at all cost.

4. It is meant to be a *short-term* stance.

You focus on self when you need external resources to support your physical existence or when you need to protect yourself. Because you are not always in danger, you only need to assume this position when a real threat exists.

As you can see, the inward-focused position is meant to be a short-term survival mechanism that we default to when we need to provide for or protect our existence. It serves a purpose that is productive when applied appropriately. However, it becomes destructive, rather than productive, when applied inappropriately. The human race understands when people act with a self-focus when it comes to survival issues; however, everyone naturally avoids inward, self-centered attitudes and actions when exposed to them in any other situation. This is where an inward focus can become problematic.

If you approach others in life with an inward focus—where self gets in the way—you create a barrier that prevents you from having your higher-level needs met. Being overly concerned with self prevents you from recognizing opportunities to contribute to others, drives others away and generally makes you unhappy. Because you don't intentionally want to make life difficult for yourself, it's important to be able to determine when you are acting with an inward focus and how to turn that focus around. The following are the most common ways in which people inadvertently create problems for themselves.

You are acting with an inward focus in the following situations:

1. When your attitudes and actions fail to consider the needs and value of others.

2. When you react to other people's actions in a way that constantly evaluates how things affect *you*.

3. When your overall attitude about life is primarily about *your own* self-satisfaction.

Let's examine each of these in more detail.

You are inward focused when your attitude and actions fail to consider the needs and value of others.

Alfred Adler, the famous psychiatrist, wrote a book entitled *What Life Should Mean to You*. In that book, he writes, "It is the individual who is not interested in his fellow men who has the greatest difficulties in life and provides the greatest injury to others. It is from among such individuals that all human failures spring." Often, it's not that we are not interested in others, but rather that our attitudes and actions give others the impression that we are not.

Essentially, inward-focused attitudes and actions do the *opposite* of what outward-focused attitudes and actions do. When outward focused, you respect, acknowledge, value and listen to other people. When inward focused, your mind is so centered on self that you are unable to recognize people's need to be valued in this way.

Inward attitudes and actions are human repellants of sorts. They drive others away from us and prevent personal fulfillment. We can neglect the needs of other people in our life in many ways; however, I have identified the six most common attitudes that serve as examples of such human repellants.

Human Repellant #1: Control over Others

The attempt to control others is driven by the desire to control and overpower other people to do what you want them to do for you. It is the unhealthy use of power tactics to get something for yourself even if it robs others of their freedom of choice, reason and rationality. It happens when you attempt to get others to do something for *you* or act in a way that they might not have freely chosen on their own. It involves being consumed with "your way" in almost every interaction you have with people, places or things.

If you attempt to control others, it's because you perceive this as the best way to get what you want and need in life. It may be the only method that has worked for you, so you employ it whenever possible. The defect with this approach is that it's an inward-focused attempt to get what you want. The results won't last, and you'll get tired and frustrated trying to achieve the outcome you want.

This inward-focused approach cannot possibly work because it violates the instincts of human nature. People feel like slaves when you try to control them, and this is the surest way to turn them against you. The bottom line is this: you can't control others. You might be able to for a short time, but eventually people will strive to correct the imbalance of power. The employee who feels controlled will find other work; the child who feels controlled will rebel; the spouse who feels controlled will withhold love. And in the meantime, these people will do what you require of them and nothing more. They will certainly not go out of their way to help you. Using this approach is the most difficult and frustrating way to attempt to get what you want and need.

Human Repellant #2: Careless Words

The words you use are powerful indicators to other people about whether or not it is safe to give to you. If your words fail to consider the needs and values of others, you run the risk of harming them and causing them to turn from you.

Words are powerful. They have the power to give life or take it away. Words have the power to encourage and meet people's deepest needs, and they also have the power to bring pain and destruction. And yet, words are so easy to say.

If you speak words without concern for how they affect the other person, if you lie to another person in order to deceive him, if you are disrespectful when you speak, you send signals to others that you cannot be trusted. If you judge, criticize or attack other people, you drive them away from you. When people feel devalued, attacked, unloved or disrespected, they distance themselves from the cause of that pain—namely, *you*. Remember, people spend their energy pursuing sources of need fulfillment. When a person feels unsafe with you because of the words you use, *it makes it difficult for them to give you what you want*. If you speak to them with words that reduce their value, they will avoid you at all costs.

> *Gentle words bring life and health; a deceitful tongue crushes the spirit.*
>
> - Proverbs 15:4

Human Repellant #3: The Scarcity Mindset

A competition is an event in which one side wins and the other side loses. People who approach life with this "win/lose" mentality believe that in order for them to "win" and get what they want, someone else must "lose." This approach requires a belief that there are limited resources for which people must compete in order to obtain as much as possible for themselves. People with this mindset take a "me against everyone else" approach to life. They believe that "the more you have the less there is for me." Although such people might not say this out loud, their actions scream the message loud and clear.

Obviously, with this kind of an approach, such a person is not able to contribute to others, and as a result, is left to "go it alone" in pursuit of the things they want. Their inward attitude drives people away and makes it unlikely that others will help them. They don't receive help, encouragement or care from others because they view others as competitors, a view that repels the very people who might otherwise be able to help them.

Human Repellant #4: An Apathetic Attitude

If you lack interest in or concern for others, you will do little to help them. Such people "can't be bothered" when someone else needs help. Give money to help the poor? What for? Let them get jobs. Help a friend move? I'd rather go golfing. Work a little extra to get the job done on time? I could care less—it's 5:00 and I'm going home to watch the game. Such an approach prevents you from contributing to the needs of others and ensures that others will not give to you in return.

Human Repellant #5: A Craving to "Get Even"

A sure sign that your thoughts have turned inward is when you catch yourself saying things like, "I'll show them," or "They won't get away with this," or "How dare they do that to me?" The primary problem with these statements is that they are all focused on how someone else has affected *you*. We say these things when we feel we have been wronged or treated unfairly, and we want to make the other person hurt like we've been hurt.

In these situations, it's not about who's right. You may be indeed right. The other person may have done something he or she should not have. But what cost are you willing to pay to get even? Is it worth it? First, if you replay in your mind how you feel you've been violated, your life becomes a daily rerun of bitter feelings, focused on how you feel. The more you contemplate the way you have been mistreated, the more you become consumed with self and your bitterness grows. When this happens, you find yourself, little by little, contemplating your own selfish ambitions and motives. This becomes a destructive trap and serves only to make *you* feel lousy.

Second, by trying to get even, we assure that we will never get ahead. Think about it. What's the surest way to get even with another person? By taking something away from them, right? For example, in a relationship, we may seek to get even with a spouse who has withheld love and affection by also withholding love and affection. As a result, we turn an unsatisfying relationship into a miserable one. Sure, we've gotten even, but at what cost?

Likewise, in an employment situation, you may attempt to get even with a cruel boss by becoming less productive. Ironically, this is the best way to ensure that you will continue to be under the thumb of this tyrant *forever*. After all, you certainly aren't going to get promoted above him by giving less than your best effort.

The only way for you to get what you want out of life is to learn to become a contributor. When you seek revenge, you have the exact opposite goal—to keep others from getting what they want. Ironically, this is one of the best ways to ensure that others won't give to you either.

Human Repellant #6: Self-absorption

Talking about yourself and your interests all the time is caused by a general lack of interest in others. Think about it: if you are truly interested in others, you would ask them how they feel, you would take an interest in their experiences and you would express concern for how events affect their lives. People who constantly talk about themselves and how situations affect them send a clear signal to others that they have little interest in anyone but themselves. Most people agree that this is not an attractive personal quality.

You are inward focused when you react to other people's actions in a way that constantly evaluates how things affect you.

Why do you still feel angry two or three hours after someone cuts you off in traffic? When someone treats you unfairly at work, why do you continue to feel mad when you get home that night? Why do you continue to feel bitter or resentful about something that happened in your life, even though it may have occurred *years* ago? The reason is that your thoughts are consumed with how these events affected *you*. You spend too much time ruminating over what happened to *you*.

Every day, you make choices in response to what is happening around you. In many cases, you face attacks, or more accurately, *perceived* attacks from those around you. These are emotional, not physical attacks (usually). For example, what emotion do you feel when you believe someone has insulted you? How do you feel when you perceive someone is being rude or disrespectful to you? How do you feel when someone cuts you off in traffic or when you discover someone has tried to cheat you? What feelings and sensations do you experience in that moment?

Usually, you won't feel very good in those situations. You might feel angry, attacked, criticized, judged, upset, hostile, fearful or anxious. These are not desirable states. As a result, you may experience pressure or tightness, which is a physiological response—your muscles, even your arteries, may constrict. You feel stress. Your body produces adrenaline, as if preparing for an attack. This response is an emotional and even metaphorical one: constriction and withdrawal of yourself from others as a way of trying to *protect yourself* physically and emotionally. This is an inward survival response. When you feel threatened like this, you turn inward to protect yourself from the *perceived* danger.

Although this inward response is natural, it is only necessary if the threat is *real*. A perceived threat need not generate this reaction. Furthermore, our bodies are only designed to accommodate this physical reaction on a short-term basis. An extended production of adrenaline and stress is very unhealthy.

In most cases in life, our inward response is not justified. The attack we object to is literally *perceived*. It's not real danger. Our perception is a result of our interpreting or judging other people's behavior. When I judge the actions of other people and interpret the meaning of an event based primarily on how it affects me, I display a remarkable loss of perspective—I fail to consider the other person, their needs and the reality of the situation.

Recently, I had an experience that demonstrated the importance of not interpreting or judging the behavior of another person. I was waiting in the checkout lane at the grocery store, when a woman came up behind me and began throwing her groceries onto the counter, all the while huffing and puffing and talking to herself. My initial thought was to turn inward and protect myself from this "crazy woman," until it dawned on me that this situation had *nothing* to do with me.

Obviously, this woman couldn't be mad at me. She didn't even know me. (People usually don't start throwing things around me until they've gotten to know me fairly well.) Therefore, rather than reacting defensively, I turned my focus outward and asked if she was okay and whether she needed help. With just the smallest amount of empathy, she immediately softened, apologized for her behavior and explained the sequence of horrible events that day that led her to act in a way she would not normally act.

By taking myself out of the equation, I'd like to think I helped to make her day a little less horrific. However, what I know is that I certainly prevented myself from becoming part of a bad situation. If I had turned to her defensively and asked, "What's your problem, lady?" I can almost guarantee that our interaction would not have been so pleasant. From that point on, she would not have been the only one having a bad day.

Even if I had not said anything to her, the incident might have affected the rest of my day—particularly if I allowed myself to become judgmental and negative. "What a wacko! This city would be a much better place to live if we just got rid of the crazy people. She's a menace!" Obviously, these kinds of thoughts are not conducive to inner peace and joy. I may have even committed the unpardonable sin of bringing this toxic waste home to my family. "Honey, you should have seen the nut I ran into at the supermarket today—the nerve of some people!" Fortunately, by not making it about me, I saved myself (and my family) this grief.

In this same way, you can avoid unnecessary stress by keeping an outward focus when interacting with your coworkers, your boss, your spouse or your friends. When you encounter a situation you *perceive* as a threat, do not judge or interpret others' actions and make the situation about you. Ask yourself, "Am I in any real danger?" Consider the validity of your response and employ compassion and empathy before you engage in any response. It's for your own good.

You are inward focused when your overall attitude about life is primarily about your own self-satisfaction.

There is nothing wrong with having the things you want in life, but if your life is *primarily* focused around your own satisfaction, you are unlikely to ever achieve any real satisfaction in the process. This is one of the supreme ironies of life. The more you focus on yourself and what you want out of life, the less likely you are to experience fulfillment.

> *If you live only for yourself, you are always in immediate danger of being bored to death with the repetition of your own views and interests.*
>
> - W. Beran Wolfe

This is a common condition for most North Americans today. Generally, we have more than ever: more vacations, more pleasures, more golf, more recreation, more entertainment, more new cars and more of whatever we could possibly imagine.

Now, you may be thinking, "What's wrong with prosperity?" There is nothing wrong with prosperity, so long as it is a *by-product* of our lives—not its sole purpose. When the central focus of our lives becomes to acquire as much as possible for ourselves, we enter a vicious cycle without end. The more we have, the more we want.

In his book *Authentic Happiness*, Martin Seligman, Ph.D., calls this condition the hedonic treadmill. He explains that even if you get everything our culture says will make you happy—fame, accomplishments, money, sex, pleasures—the satisfaction will not last. For a brief moment, it will seem like getting these things brings happiness. Yet in the end, it doesn't lead to any lasting satisfaction. Seligman puts it this way:

> *Another barrier to raising your level of happiness is the "hedonic treadmill."… As you accumulate more material possessions and accomplishments, your expectations rise. The deeds and things you worked so hard for no longer make you happy; you need to get something even better to boost your level of happiness into the upper reaches of its set range. But once you get the next possession or achievement, you adapt to it as well, and so on.[27]*

We see the hedonic treadmill at work in the lives of many young people today. Youth growing up in this me generation have little understanding of what it means to contribute. As a result, they have everything anyone could ever want, except, sadly, satisfaction. How do we know? Suicide is the third leading cause of death among those 15 to 24 years old. Among young people aged 10 to 14 years, the rate has doubled in the last two decades.[28]

The reason happiness is not found in a life focused on self-satisfaction is that such a life has little room for contribution. If you overextend your focus on self in this way, your attitudes and actions will rarely consider how your life may serve others. A life that does not contribute to something beyond itself leads to discontent and, in many cases, depression. By centering our lives on our own self-satisfaction, we violate the *Law of Contribution* and end up with less of the life we crave most.

A life directed chiefly toward the fulfillment of personal desires sooner or later always leads to bitter disappointment.

- Albert Einstein

Conclusion

These are the ways you may become inward focused. If you consider each of these factors, you will notice that you are not at all attracted to people who display these inward characteristics. In the same way, people will avoid you when you display such inward attitudes and actions.

An inward focus does not produce the results we want in life. When you are inward, you fail to contribute, people in your life fail to get their needs met, you don't get what you want, and everyone feels lousy in the process. So why do we act this way? Most often it's because we fail to see how our short-term decisions are connected to the results we get later in life. The next chapter provides you with examples that illustrate this truth.

Chapter 6
I Didn't Ask for This!

On Sunday, June 13, 2004, Matt Starr was at Ameriquest Field in Arlington, Texas, watching the home team Rangers take on the St. Louis Cardinals. When a foul ball was hit toward where he was sitting, the 28-year-old landscaper leapt over the seat in front of him. Even though the ball had landed at the feet of four-year-old Nicholas O'Brien, Starr knocked the boy against the seats and pounced on the ball. Observing this incredible act of selfishness, fans objected and began chanting, "Give the boy the ball." But greedily clutching the ball, Starr returned to his seat, unwilling to part with his new souvenir.

Unfortunately for Starr, he had no idea how people react to such selfish actions. Almost immediately, a series of retaliations were launched from all corners. The ballplayers who witnessed Starr's actions were repulsed. Between innings, Cardinals' outfielder Reggie Sanders went into the stands to give the boy a bat. Nicholas also received souvenirs from the Texas Rangers, including one signed by Hall of Fame pitcher Nolan Ryan.

Even worse, video of Starr's boorish behavior was shown on evening newscasts across the country. As if that were not enough, the television program *Good Morning America* picked up the story, interviewing the boy's mother and further exposing Starr's incredible act of greed.

Four embarrassing days later, Starr publicly expressed sorrow for his behavior. He agreed to send a letter of apology to the O'Brien family, along with the ball and tickets for the entire family to attend a future Rangers' game.

Is this an unusual response to selfish behavior? Not really. Consider this equally entertaining story.

Best-selling author Gil Beers, while at Forest Lawn Memorial Garden in California, asked an employee, "What was the most expensive funeral you ever had here?" Despite presiding over countless funerals, the employee easily remembered the recipient of a lavish send-off.

The deceased was embittered with his ex-wife and children. In his will, he had left them almost nothing, but instead, had provided $200,000 for an ostentatious farewell. He purchased a bronze casket for around $18,000, and a beautiful rose window was created for $25,000. Amazingly, even after these and other expenditures, the mortuary still had about $100,000 left to spend, so they lined his gravesite with orchids—$100,000 worth!

The orchids, in and of themselves, must have been a sight to behold. It's probably a shame that only three people got to see it. That's right. Apparently, this man had been as selfish in life as he had been in death. As a result, only three of the thousands of people he must have met during his lifetime felt the need to attend his funeral. And I suspect that one or two of them may have shown up just to make sure he was really dead.

He who lives only to benefit himself confers on the world a benefit when he dies.

- Tertullian

As you can see, inward-focused actions really are a human repellant. They not only keep people away from you (in life and in death) but they turn others against you. As a result, with an inward focus it is difficult to achieve the things we all want in life because other people are reluctant to invest their time, energy, emotion, love and resources into a selfish person.

As a result, any type of inward-focused action, however unintentional, may create barriers that make it difficult for you to get what you want. We don't like people who are selfish. Stop for a minute and think of someone you really don't like or respect. Get a clear picture of that person and consider why you don't like him or her. Regarding such people, the answer will always come back to their attitude or actions being inward focused—selfish. They might be greedy, unfair, talk about themselves all the time, do things that are inconsiderate of others (like Matt Starr), be controlling, and so on. Now, as you contemplate that person and his or her actions let me ask you this: would you go out of your way to help him or her? Not likely. When people act in a selfish manner, it creates barriers between them and others. If you live with an inappropriate focus on self, you might find the results you get in life are not what you hoped for.

The "All about Me" Barrier

To illustrate, let's consider the true story of a young girl. For this purpose, let's call her Inward Irene. Irene is an attractive, talented and smart young woman—just the type of person you would expect to go on to lead a productive and fulfilling life. She has everything going for her except for one small thing—her inward focus is producing the opposite results from what she is hoping for. As a result, at the age of 19, Irene suffers from depression and an ongoing stretch of "bad luck." While her future should be bright, it is actually quite dim.

While Irene certainly had the ability to do well in school, she never quite lived up to her potential. Whenever she faced difficulty in a class, she blamed the teacher for her failure. She focused on how the teacher caused her grief. As a result, she alienated the people who were best able (and most willing) to help her. Or, in other words, she created a barrier to getting what she could have otherwise achieved.

Irene took a similar inward approach in dealing with her classmates. She judged other people harshly because of how *she* perceived them. If there was a disagreement, Irene focused on what the other person did to *her*. She ruminated over past disputes and how her classmates had offended *her*. It even got to the point where she no longer enjoyed dance class—a class that she normally enjoyed—because she did not "like" some of the other girls in that class. In her mind, those people offended *her*. By focusing on herself and how others affected her, she distanced herself more and more from her classmates. In the end, she graduated from high school with very few (if any) close friends.

Even after high school, Irene continued to struggle with friendships. She made new friends, but never kept them very long. When asked why, she blamed the breakdown in the relationship on the other person. "She's so annoying!" "He was a jerk to me!" In short, she continued to see others as the problem.

Selfishness is not living as one wishes to live; it is asking others to live as one wishes to live.

                                              - Oscar Wilde

After high school, she entered the workforce—albeit with the same inward focus. She failed to see other people's perspectives and focused only on how things made *her* feel. At each new job, she focused on how *unfair* everyone and everything was to *her*. Her work assignments were *unfair*. Her work schedule was *unfair*. The customers were *unfair*. The pay was *unfair*. She called in sick whenever she did not feel like working. She treated her customers rudely if she felt they "deserved" it.

Not surprisingly, with her constant griping, absences and rude behavior to customers, she soon found herself looking for a new job. She went from job to job, almost always getting fired or being asked to leave because she refused to meet the needs of her coworkers, her bosses and their customers. And with each job termination, it became increasingly difficult for her to get a new job. No one was willing to help such a selfish person.

Therefore, at the tender age of 19, with an entire world of possibilities in front of her, Irene was becoming increasingly negative and depressed. She was lonely and struggling financially. Instead of enjoying what should have been the best time of her life, she was living a nightmare. Inadvertently, she had allowed her inward focus to blur the prospects for her future.

The tragic irony here is that Irene's situation was not due to neglect or disinterest. Irene was extremely interested in herself. In fact, that was the very nature of her problem. She was so obsessed with herself and how everything and everyone affected *her* that she drove everyone who may have helped her away. She drove her teachers away. She drove her friends away. She drove her employers away. As a result, Irene's all-consuming interest with Irene led to Irene getting exactly the opposite of what she wanted for herself.

Sadly, the real problem for such people is that they have no idea that it's *their* inward focus that is preventing them from having the life they want. Without an understanding of the *Law of Contribution*, people like Irene fail to get their real needs met. Their intense inward focus produces the opposite from the result they really want. In some cases, the results can be destructive and can affect the lives of others as well. Let's take, for example, the true story of Selfish Sam (obviously, not his real name).

The Barrier of Self-serving Actions

Sam was 42 years old, a husband and the father of two children. And while Sam loved his family, he loved Sam even more. As a result, he spent the vast majority of his free time in activities that were focused on him, not considering the needs of his family. He golfed three or four times a week, spent evenings after work with his buddies and generally did all of the things that *he* wanted to do, including having the occasional affair while away on business.

Interestingly, for the longest time, Sam didn't notice any negative effects of his selfish actions. He was enjoying a life built solely upon the gratification of his own desires. Or so he thought.

What he was not noticing was that his wife and children were growing increasingly distant from him. Although he was providing for their basic needs for food, clothing, shelter and the like, he was not meeting their most basic need—the need to feel loved. After all, it's hard to convince people you love them when what you love most is spending time away from them.

The distance between Sam and his wife only widened when she discovered one of his affairs. Without the glue of love to hold their relationship together, she decided to file for divorce. As often happens, the divorce proved especially painful for the children. Their grades suffered and they began exhibiting some troubling new behaviors.

And Sam's troubles were just beginning. The divorce hurt him financially as well as emotionally. His wife received half of their assets in the divorce. He had to take a second mortgage on his house to pay her the equity that was due to her. He also began making spousal and child support payments. Almost overnight, his financial obligations had increased exponentially. To make matters worse, his performance on his job was beginning to suffer as he found it difficult to concentrate.

In Sam's effort to "have it all," he ended up with *nothing*. He lost the love and companionship of his wife. He lost half of their assets. He lost the respect of his children. And Sam was not the only loser in this case. His children suffered the pain of the divorce. His wife found it difficult to trust again. Sam and everyone he loved paid a high price for his inward focus—a price that was directly correlated with his self-centered actions.

Barriers Created by Judgment

There are yet other ways an inward focus can cause more trouble for us than we'd like. Judgment of others is one of the most destructive inward attitudes. When you judge others, you become inward focused because judgment requires that you view another person's action and interpret how those actions affect *you*. When you judge people, you drive them away from you.

Let's take the case of Peter and Laurie. These young lovers were married for two years, during which they had frequent arguments. These arguments often resulted from judgment caused by misinterpretation. For example, one summer evening, Peter and Laurie attended a sporting event. As they sat in the stands watching the game, a man and woman walked up the bleachers toward them. The man was carrying a rather large duffle bag, which struck Peter as being unusual—and even somewhat alarming. For that reason, his eyes remained fixed on the couple as they took their seats.

Laurie observed Peter gazing at the couple and assumed Peter was fixated on the young, attractive woman who was with the man. Offended by Peter's actions, she felt jealousy and anger. She didn't say anything, but instead, focused her thoughts on Peter's "boorish and insensitive" behavior for the rest of the game. On the way home, Peter sensed some indifference in Laurie's behavior and asked her if something was wrong. He then received the full expression of anger and resentment caused by Laurie's misinterpretation of that one short event. As a result, what should have been a pleasant evening for the young couple was ruined by yet *another* fight.

Obviously, this fight was completely unnecessary. It was caused by Laurie's judgment of her husband's actions and her interpretation of how those actions affected *her*. As a result, Laurie spent the entire time at the game thinking about "what a pig" Peter was. Even worse, she caused further divisions in their already troubled relationship. After all, Peter, who in this case did nothing wrong, is far less likely to want to attend another event with Laurie, fearing that he will be accused again of ogling other women.

While this example involved an overly jealous wife, husbands often react similarly. In fact, if we're honest with ourselves, we must confess that there is a little Laurie in all of us. It's a natural response to our innate need for security. Our nervous system is wired to be on alert for possible threats to what we value most. Yet the problem in this case was not a real threat. Laurie's inward focus caused her to inappropriately judge her husband by misinterpreting how a certain event might affect *her*. But there was no real threat to the relationship.

For instance, Laurie observed that her husband was looking in the direction of the couple. She couldn't determine exactly what Peter was looking at, so she simply filled in the blanks. She could have just as easily concluded he was looking at the man or even something in the stands around them. Unfortunately, she chose to let her insecurities get the better of her and concluded that Peter must have been watching the other woman.

People with an inward focus make this kind of mistake often. Why? Because they tend to filter every event in life through the lens of "How does this affect *me*?" As a result, they are a lot more likely to find perceived threats to their security and well-being. How could they not?

Now, I will admit it is sometimes hard not to question the intention of other people when they say or do something you don't understand. However, if you find you are frequently upset with other people because of their actions, the problem is likely *you*. If others often offend you, or if you are often defensive because of others' actions, you are unfairly interpreting and judging other people's behavior. Watch out! You're turning inward and it will only be a matter of time before you suffer the consequences.

When you act this way, you drive people away from you, making it difficult to get what you want and need from others. When a person feels judged, it makes it difficult for him or her to give you what you want, even if the person would otherwise want to do so.

How did things end up for Laurie? It became increasingly difficult for her husband to meet her innate need for love while being judged by her. Without the intimacy required in a marriage, the relationship deteriorated and eventually ended like many others do— in divorce. So while Laurie's actions were driven by her need to keep her husband, her inward-focused actions served to drive him away. In the end, she did not exactly get what she wanted.

Irene, Sam and Laurie are just a few examples of people who have learned the hard way that you don't get the results you want when you approach life with an inward focus. Their failures are clear. There are other, less obvious ways in which an inward focus can produce disheartening results. We all know people who somehow beat the odds and reach some level of external success despite their selfish ways. These people, however, do not escape the effects of the *Law of Contribution*.

The Barrier of Self-satisfaction

When you are focused simply on satisfying your own desires, and not on contributing to others, you end up with less satisfaction, not more. As a result, you gain everything you think you want but none of what you *need*. Your success brings temporary satisfaction, but it produces an empty result. It's like eating food but not receiving any nourishment.

If we're not careful, we can end up like the ill-fated explorers, Burke and Wills, who attempted to cross Australia in 1861. Along their journey, they ran into an aboriginal group who served them cake made from the seeds of the nardu plant. Later in their journey, when they had run out of food, they attempted to sustain themselves solely by eating nardu. They later learned (albeit too late) that the nardu is filling, but it contains no nutritional value. Within a period of three weeks, both men literally starved to death, despite eating up to four pounds of nardu per day. Here is an entry from Will's journal a few days before his death:

> *I am weaker than ever although I have a good appetite and relish the nardu much but it seems to give us no nutriment...but starvation on nardu is by no means very unpleasant but for the weakness one feels and the utter inability to move oneself, for as far as appetite is concerned, it gives me the greatest satisfaction....*[29]

Many people could say the same thing about their consumption of money, titles, looks, sex and every kind of pleasure available. All of these things give great satisfaction, but no nutrition. In other words, these things will make you feel full, but they will not make you feel *fulfilled*. Ironically, when people focus their lives solely on *self*-satisfaction, they end up with no real *satisfaction* at all. The end result of such an inward focus is the *opposite* of what the person is pursuing.

Some renowned men and women of our time have had to learn this lesson the hard way. Take the example of Ernest Hemingway. He did everything a man born in 1899 could ever dream or imagine. He sipped champagne in Paris. He enjoyed bullfights in Spain. He went on well-publicized game hunts in Africa and hunted grizzly bears in America's northwest. And, of course, he had a distinguished literary career. Yet at the age of 61—after a life of wine, women and song—Hemingway fell victim to his inward-focused life. He chose to end his life, leaving a note accurately describing how people feel when their life is primarily focused on their own self-satisfaction. The note read, "Life is one [expletive] thing after another."

Consider the strikingly similar example of one of the most innovative businessmen in the world—Howard Hughes. This man's business accomplishments are staggering. It's hard to discern fact from folklore, but even if it's fiction, it's worth considering. According to different sources, Hughes acquired his father's company, the Hughes Corporation, at the age of 19. Later, he bought RKO Pictures and had a large stake in TWA, which netted him half-a-billion dollars when he was ousted because of some irregularities in running the company. In fact, he had a hand in creating many businesses that exist to this day.

Yet at the time of his death, he hadn't been seen for 20 years. The FBI had to take his fingerprints to identify his corpse. And while he had married actress Jean Peters and dated Ava Gardner, Lana Turner and some of the most beautiful women of Hollywood, he died alone with hypodermic needles embedded in his skin from his injections of codeine.

The pursuit of happiness is a most ridiculous phrase; if you pursue happiness you'll never find it.

- C. P. Snow

Hemingway and Hughes are just two examples of rich and famous people who learned too late that all of the fame, fortune and accolades in the world are not enough to create a fulfilling life. What might their lives have been like if they had learned to channel some of their energy toward the needs of others? Likely, very different.

True fulfillment is only possible when we obtain the things we want as a *result* of our contributions in life. Living life with a "get all I can for me" attitude is actually a "me against the world" contest, in which you are bound to lose.

As unintentional as our inward focus may be, we'll suffer the results of such actions all the same. If you find there are aspects of your life where you are not getting the results you want, you may want to contemplate a change of focus. It's only by understanding the *Law of Contribution* and learning how to become outward focused that you can purposefully take action to produce what you really want most for yourself and for others in your life. The next chapter will provide powerful examples of how a purposeful outward focus can ensure healthy, lasting results in your life, very often in ways you might not expect.

Chapter 7
Maybe This Really Works!

Paradox: a statement or proposition that seems self-contradictory or absurd but in reality expresses a possible truth.

This is the *Law of Contribution*. The paradox is that you actually get what *you* want by focusing on meeting the needs of others *first*. Yes, it sounds absurd, but in reality it expresses a real truth. In real life, it does work. It sounds idealistic, but the truth is, it is the most practical and logical approach to achieving what you want. Whether you are coaching a team to win, motivating employees, or raising children, the *Law of Contribution* is the foundational principle that must guide all actions if you are to succeed. To help make this idea more real, consider some real-life examples of the *Law of Contribution* at work.

The world of college, semi-pro and professional sports represents one of the most competitive environments in which a person can work. Coaches are charged with the task of training and leading teams that have only one objective: to win. In many (most) cases, they don't get to keep their jobs for long if they don't produce that result. Today, most coaches last only three to five years with a typical franchise sports team.

As a result, a coach has a personal objective and desire: to produce a team that wins. How might a coach use the *Law of Contribution* to get what he wants? At first glance, it would appear that contributing to the needs of his players would have very little to do with coaching a winning team. However, the *Law of Contribution* works in all aspects of life. Let's see how.

Most professionals would agree that many of the players competing in professional sports are capable of similarly high levels of play. The difference in the level of actual talent between players is marginal. How, then, does a coach get the most from both his individual players and his players as a team? The question becomes, does the coach approach his players with an inward approach or an outward approach? What's the difference?

The coach has an objective that *he* wants to achieve: to win games. When the coach focuses on what *he* wants, his approach is inward and might look something like this.

Practices are about preparation for the next game. They are about getting the players to conform to the coach's game plan. They are about driving the players to perform. Due to this short-term "give me what I want" outlook, the players feel good when they win and bad when they lose. The coach might get angry when they lose and players certainly feel the pressure when things are not going well. With this approach, the players feel like they are constantly being driven to win at all costs (they are!).

You might think that such an approach is what sport is all about and that what I have described is perfectly normal. However, you'll notice that in sport, very few coaches stay with one team for extended periods of time. Only a few teams actually "get" what I'm about to explain next. The truth is that teams with long, impressive winning records are teams that take an outward approach to coaching.

With an outward-focused approach, the coaching focus of practice is not only about preparing for the next game, but also about player development. Practices are about giving the players the direction and instruction they need to become *better each time they play.* This attitude is about meeting the players' need to feel significant and valued because of their own personal achievement and growth. When people feel they are achieving and growing by their own efforts, they become stronger individuals and more and more capable. By focusing on what *players* need, the players learn to perform at their highest level.

With an outward approach, although the coach wants to win, he or she focuses on teaching players the importance of contributing their *very best* effort in each and every practice and game. By focusing on what matters—the players' personal development—the opportunity to win each game becomes greater because the players are pushing to play at their highest level.

With this approach, players do not judge the result of the game by the score—rather, they judge it by whether or not they feel they contributed their very best effort. Ironically, this team wins more games than the team focused on the short-term win. The players on this team feel a purpose in what they do beyond the short-term win.

In case you are beginning to think this is an idealistic approach, consider the real-life example of one coach who understood the significance of this approach. He was one of the most winning coaches of all time: John Wooden, the basketball coaching legend. Wooden coached the UCLA Bruins basketball team for nearly a quarter century and set records that are still unmatched. He created a dynasty in college basketball. He won ten national NCAA championships in 12 years. His team from 1972–1974 played two perfect seasons—88 games without a loss. Never in college basketball history had this been done, and it hasn't been done since.

How did he do it? Although Wooden did not necessarily understand that his actions were "outward focused," or that his coaching style complied with the *Law of Contribution*, his approach was exactly what I have explained above.

In his book *My Personal Best*, Wooden said, "Some have suggested that one of the reasons UCLA often outscored opponents was that I never stressed outscoring opponents—that is, 'beating' someone else or 'needing' to win a game.... Try your hardest, make the effort, do your best. That's what I stressed..."[30]

He said, "the 'score' that matters most is the one that measures your effort—and ultimately, only you know the score." John Wooden defined success as "peace of mind, which is a direct result of self-satisfaction in knowing you did your best to become the best that you are capable of becoming."[31]

"I never talked about winning or beating an opponent. My job, and the team's job, was to get us as close to being as good as we could get. The final score would be a by-product of that effort."[32]

It is never simply a case of win or lose, because I do not demand victory. The significance of the score is secondary to the importance of finding out how good you can be.[33]

- John Wooden

Clearly, Wooden's approach was not about what *he* wanted; it was about player development and coaching in such a way that each player had his personal needs met. By focusing on players' needs, he was able to develop players who learned to play at their highest level. People always perform their best when their needs are met. That approach proved to be successful in beating teams that focused on the short-term win.

Fortunately, UCLA gave him the opportunity to prove his theory because Wooden coached basketball at UCLA for *15 years* before the team won a national championship. That's right, 15 years without an NCAA championship! Yet the long-term result was a dynasty that will never be forgotten. What's even more significant is not the "wins" in the game of basketball, but the "wins" in the game of life for those he coached. His players will attest to the significant impact that Wooden made on their life. When you contribute to others, when you live your life helping others meet their needs, you get what you want, and your life becomes significant in ways you cannot anticipate.

The same approach is just as valid in any other sector of life. Business is no different. Business owners want to "win" at their game in the same way that coaches want to "win" at theirs. Just like a sports team, a business also has its best chance of success when it meets the needs of its people. However, a business that is inward-focused has little chance of winning.

When a business is inward focused, its leaders focus on the short-term performance of its people rather than on meeting needs. Inward-focused leaders ask, "What can I get from my employees?" not "What can I contribute?" As a natural result, employees feel like they are simply being used for the company's own benefit. They are paid just enough, but not generously. They are rarely recognized for the value they bring. They are treated simply as workers, who work. The company focuses on what it wants from the employee. Employee performance reviews are one-sided, rating employees on how well they have "performed." Rarely does the company ask, "What do you need to do your job better?" As a result, most employees leave their job because of lack of appreciation. That's a fact!

An outward-focused business focuses on what the employees' most fundamental needs are, and the primary task of its leaders is to contribute toward helping their employees meet these needs.

Employees need to feel valued for what they do. They need to achieve and develop as individuals in order to feel their best. Real leaders "coach" their employees so they have the opportunity to perform their best, to achieve and to grow.

Employers who focus on meeting their employees' needs take four specific actions to foster the personal development of employees and make them feel valued:

1. They recognize and reward employees' contributions. This sounds simplistic, but few actually do this.

2. They provide employees with the opportunity to achieve and accomplish. They do this by identifying the employees' greatest skills and assigning tasks and responsibilities that enable the exercise of those skills. The benefit is two-fold. First, by using their greatest skills, employees are able to offer the employer their greatest contributions. Second, employees develop and grow their most valuable talents and feel their best. Employees, like athletes, learn to perform at their best and the company ultimately wins.

3. They set targets employees can achieve so their sense of achievement is met. When employees achieve, they feel empowered to perform at even higher levels.

4. They turn employee performance reviews into mutual goal-setting sessions in which employees see their opportunity for growth and personal development.

When employees are treated this way, their sense of value is heightened and they are better able to perform so the company can achieve its objectives. In his book *Winning*, Jack Welch says, "Self-confidence energizes, and it gives your people the courage to stretch, take risks, and achieve beyond their dreams. It's the fuel of a winning team."[34] Welch says that from his experience he understands that "...people inherently and instinctively want to be respected for their work and effort and individuality."[35] In other words, they want their need for significance met.

The importance of treating people in this humane way is nothing new to great business leaders such as Doug McGregor, Peter Drucker and Ken Blanchard. They have all extolled the importance of valuing the human person in the workplace. However, understanding it in the context of the *Law of Contribution* helps identify the value it offers to both the employee and organization. It helps us understand why the *Law of Contribution* states, "*You get what you want when you give to meet others' needs.*" Using this as a guiding principle in the workplace can help any business get the results it wants and needs most.

Such an approach works in sports, in business and equally well at home. Consider the example of raising children. When it comes to raising kids, there are things that *you want* as a parent. All parents want their children to grow up to achieve and be successful. Like everything else in life, you can attempt to do this with an inward approach, or you can do it with an outward approach. Although in both cases the end result *you* want is what's best for your children, in only one of these cases is the end result what you really hoped for.

When you raise your children with an inward-focused approach, you are focused on the end result—success—rather than on your children's development. You push your children to achieve and believe that by setting the standards high, your children can get there. You reprimand your children when they get bad grades, but praise your children when they get good grades. You praise them when they play well in their sporting events, but express your displeasure when they fail to play to their ability. In these responses, you make your children feel loved and accepted when they meet your expectations, but unloved and unacceptable when they feel they have disappointed you.

The result is that your children experience unnecessary stress when they sense the need to achieve in order to be accepted, feel significant and loved. In other words, their needs are *conditionally* met, based on their performance. When this happens, they feel fear that they will not be good enough. They also feel insecure because if they do not produce what *you* want or expect, their need to be accepted, valued and loved does not get met. As a result, stress builds in their lives and although outwardly they appear to be doing well, inside they are learning that in order to get what they want, they must go hard. This fear follows them throughout their lives, and although it might drive them to succeed, true happiness and fulfillment are not easily found.

Madeline is a 31-year-old woman who is absolutely gorgeous, yet suffers from an extreme case of insecurity. She is driven to succeed and to look good. Externally, people would see her as "having it all together." She is smart, beautiful and an achiever. Yet surprisingly, she has never really been happy in life. Furthermore, her sense of insecurity caused ongoing problems in her marriage. Finally, desperate for a solution, she sought help from a counselor, who helped her identify the problem. Here are her exact words about the discovery: "I actually had talked to the counselor about this—she was good about unraveling my past and indicated that my dad's pressure to be *the best* at everything (although his intentions were good), put extreme pressure on me (and my brother and sister)—which in turn made us very afraid of failure—created insecurity, and developed a pattern of lying when we thought we might disappoint." She said she thinks this result is quite common among kids whose parents put too much pressure on them.

If you have children and are concerned that they grow up to be the best possible adults they can be, then your role is not to tell them what to do, but first and foremost to *affirm* them. What children need most is *affirmation of their value*. When this happens, they will certainly grow up to be accomplishing and successful citizens.

Raising children with an outward-focused approach produces a much healthier result.

Children are healthiest when their need for love is met. Parents' primary purpose is to provide their child with *unconditional* love.

If you focus on loving your children regardless of what they do or achieve, the chances of them growing up to achieve and succeed *and be happy* are far greater.

If you love your children unconditionally, they will not be afraid to try things and fail, because when they fail, they will not be at risk of feeling unloved or rejected. This provides them with the freedom to try new things and eventually succeed. When they feel loved despite failure, they feel safe to try again, because if they fail, their value will not be threatened.

Parents are like basketball coaches helping their children experience things that enable their successful achievement of tasks by their own effort. Parents, like business leaders, help provide opportunities for their children's personal growth. Children are taught that life is about them making their best effort. Failures are not seen as personal failure, but learning experiences that help them develop.

When you love your children unconditionally, they are the happiest, healthiest and most successful they can possibly be. The best results are obtained by focusing outward, on your children's needs, rather than inward, on what you want. By not focusing on obtaining what you want, but rather by focusing on the development of your children, you can meet their needs and obtain a true win-win that produces healthy, life-long results. Once again, "*You get what you want when you give to meet others' needs.*"

These are but a few examples of how to employ the principles of the *Law of Contribution* in everyday life. It's only when you contribute to the needs of those in your life that you can really get what you want. It's only when you approach life with an outward focus that you can meet other people's needs in such a way that both they and you reap the true rewards life has to offer. This really does work!

Chapter 8
Why Is It So Easy for Them?

If you're like me, you've probably read countless books that provide a variety of "steps to success." Most commonly, you'll hear things like, "Set Goals, Work Hard, Don't Give Up." For years it seemed like I was working hard, but not meeting with the end results I ultimately desired. Perhaps you are in the same position.

However, unless you start with an understanding of the *Law of Contribution*, you're not likely to get the results you really want. If you're not outward focused, success will be a difficult achievement. People who reach high levels of success in life seem to innately understand this *Law of Contribution*. It's no coincidence that when those who have real success and happiness in life are interviewed, a common theme is revealed. Successful people do set goals and do work hard; however, highly successful individuals also understand the need to be outward focused.

Successful People Surround Themselves with Success

Successful people purposefully contribute to others in order to help people accomplish their objectives. Why do they want to help others succeed? Because they understand that by helping others accomplish their objectives, those people become stronger and more skilled. As a result, the already-successful person becomes surrounded by stronger, more skilled people. Then they have strong resources upon which they can draw later in life, which enhances their opportunity for future achievement. The mutual "give and take" facilitates growth both ways. In this way, contributors literally surround themselves with success. They can do this because they don't see other people as threats—they see other people as resources. This is true of very high achievers.

Most people do not understand this principle because they are busy trying to *get* for themselves, rather than to *give* to others. Most people don't recognize that you must first give before you can get.

The more of these mutually satisfying relationships that you are able to develop, the easier it will be to achieve your objectives. When successful people need to get something done, it is much easier for them than for the average person. Why? It's easier because they have the ability to call on any one of their many resource points to help them. Here is a simple example.

I have a friend named Harold who is a headhunter—a recruiter of sales and management staff. OK, that's not his real name, but let's call him Harold the Headhunter. I met Harold years ago when I was looking for work myself. He did not end up placing me; however, during our interview, he treated me with great respect and a bond was created between us. Not long after, I was a manager of a company and needed to hire a new employee. Guess whom I called? That's right, Harold. He found a suitable employee for our company. The result was that he earned a commission and I obtained the employee I needed. This was a fair business transaction. But it did not end there.

Harold maintained contact with me and we developed some common interests. He invited me to join him for a game of golf a few times a year. I would return the favor and invite him when I was playing with business colleagues—especially when there was opportunity for him to meet other business professionals. As time went on, Harold would call me from time to time for advice, and I knew I could do the same. Whenever I needed new employees, I would call Harold and he would provide the necessary assistance. It would appear as though this was nothing more than a common business relationship of giving and taking. But it proved to be more.

A special bond was created because we both knew that each of us would go out of our way to help the other. Time had proven this to be true. When our industry got very busy, finding employees was not just tough, it became a serious barrier to growth. Due to the relationship I had with Harold, our company was introduced to well-qualified workers who were available for employment before any other companies had the opportunity to hire them. When other companies needed employees, they had to place ads in the paper, sort through hundreds of resumes, spend hours sifting through the "duds," and even more time interviewing candidates, hoping to eventually find someone that they hoped could do the job.

In our case, during a casual conversation with Harold, I advised him that our company was continuing to grow and one day soon would require the addition of a senior salesperson. However, our industry was very specialized, and as a result, well-qualified and experienced sales professionals were in short supply. Within a month, Harold had come into contact with exactly the right person that we needed and we had "first dibs" on him. He was experienced and ideal for the job. We hired him without delay.

My relationship with Harold, based on mutual contributing, made this possible. What is most important to recognize about this story is how *all individuals involved* got their needs met and how easy the process was. Our company obtained what it needed: a senior-level, experienced salesperson who helped grow our business. I received access to this person as the result of a brief conversation with Harold. The new salesperson contributed to our sales, which improved my personal income because I was paid on overall growth. Harold was paid for yet another placement, which took very little of his time. The new salesperson landed an ideal position without having to hand out a single resume. We all got our needs met with very little effort. This is how easy it can be to get results when you have these kinds of relationships in your life.

Of course, in order to have such relationships, you need to learn to approach life with an outward focus. You need to learn to genuinely care about other people and help meet their needs. Successful people who are this way naturally build strong relationships in many aspects of life.

George Lucas is one such successful person. He has reached the pinnacle of success in his industry. He is the creator of *Star Wars* and has revolutionized the art of motion pictures. He confirms that helping others was a key to his success and the success of his colleagues:

> *Part of the reason my friends and I became successful is that we were always helping each other. If I got a job, I would help somebody else get a job. If somebody got more successful than me, it was partly my success. My success wasn't based on how I could push down everyone around me. My success was based on how much I could push everybody up. And eventually their success was the same way. And in the process they pushed me up, and I pushed them up, and we kept doing that, and we still do that.*[36]

He affirms that the common characteristic of successful people is the ability to be outward focused: "I don't think there's anyone who's become successful who doesn't understand how important it is to... help other people...."[37]

Quincy Jones tells a similar story. After 50 years in show business, he stands alone as the most nominated Grammy artist of all time, with 76 nominations. He has composed over 50 major motion picture and television scores, earned international acclaim as producer of the historic *We Are the World* recording (one of the best-selling singles of all time) and produced Michael Jackson's best-selling album *Thriller*. He talks about how he received help from others, and how he gives back in the same way:

> *A lot of the guys were like that...they just took me under their wing, and that's why I automatically help young people. I just love it, because they did that for me. They were there.*[38]

Tom Peters, in his book *Re-Imagine!*, provides an example of how successful people develop strong relationships and resource points with other people. How? By recognizing others. He says,

> *I had a boss in Washington years ago. Insanely busy. But on Day One of working with him, I observed that he closed his office door at about 7:00 p.m. for a half-hour. He religiously spent those 30 minutes dictating (that's what we did back then) a dozen or more simple "thank-you's" to people he'd met during the day. People who had "gotten him a meeting" with someone he needed to see or who made a supportive comment when he really needed it. Result (no overstatement): He had a slavish network of devotees throughout D.C.*[39]

Successful people are known to bring others along in their pursuit of achievement. As a result, people trust them. I know one such man personally. His name is Ernie the Entrepreneur (do I really need to say that that's not his real name?) He is enormously successful. What is most interesting is that he has been successful at just about everything he has done. Some have said, "Everything he touches turns to gold." Yet many of his successful businesses have been so diverse that one wonders how one person could do so well in such a wide variety of businesses.

How does he do it? He has relationships that provide him with all the resources he needs for success. He started a finance company that required millions of investment dollars. No problem for Ernie. He made phone calls to people he knew, and they gladly participated. Why? Because they know Ernie takes care of others.

He started another company in the cement business. What did he know about cement? Nothing, but he knew other people who knew the cement business. He was able to hire top-level personnel at a time when good people were hard to find. Then later, he needed to raise $20 million to help grow the business. He did it in two days. He lives in a circle of interdependent relationships that make his success look *easy* to the average person.

This attitude of taking care of others is seen commonly in highly successful leaders. Ernie is no exception. Sanford I. Weill, a great financier, shares this same outward attitude. When Sanford Weill first looked for work on Wall Street, he had no great connections, and his parents in Brooklyn were certainly not wealthy. In spite of these obstacles, he built the second largest company in the financial services industry—Shearson Lehman Brothers.

When asked, "What contribution that you've made do you feel is the most important?" his answer reflected his desire to help others along the way. He said,

*Things I've done that have really been good have been very
diverse. From the business point of view, always encouraging
the people in our company to own stock in the company, and
if we're going to build something great, to have a lot of people share in the benefits of that greatness. A lot of people at
Shearson ended up making a lot of money because they had
stock or stock options. Their kids were able to go to college,
and it changed a lot of people's lives.*[40]

Frederick Smith, founder of Federal Express, speaks in a similar way about helping others. When asked, "What do you think
your most important traits have been in achieving what you have
done?" his answer was consistent with other outward leaders:

*I've been very interested in the people who I work with
being successful as well. I don't think we have many people
who've worked at FedEx, particularly in the executive ranks,
who don't have good feelings about the company. I hope
that's because they feel they were treated fairly and got their
shot at glory and opportunity. I think that's a big part of it.
To make sure that the people you're working with have a
chance to be successful.*[41]

Success and Humility

Humility is one of the greatest virtues common among highly
successful people. Humility is an outward-focused virtue because
it considers others as equal to, or as more important than, the
"self." The most powerful leaders understand this principle.

Jim Collins, in his book *Good to Great*, surveyed CEOs of great
companies and found humility as a common characteristic among
these leaders. Their attitude said, "It's not about me." They understood that the needs of others come before the needs of self.

Dr. Maya Angelou worked with Martin Luther King, Jr., at the height of the civil rights movement. When Dr. Angelou was interviewed by the Academy of Achievement and was asked, "What was Dr. King really like, personally?" she affirmed that humility was one of the virtues of this great man:

> Dr. King was really humble so that he was accessible to everybody. The smallest child could come up to him, the most powerful person could come up to him, he never changed. If somebody very rich and very powerful said, "Dr. King, I want to speak to you," he was the same person to that person as he would be to one of you who is 16, 17.... He was still accessible, gentle, powerful, humble.[42]

> Everyone who exalts himself will be humbled, and he who humbles himself will be exalted.

> - Jesus

The *Law of Contribution* is a reality. An outward focus always produces growth for the giver. It worked for Ernie the Entrepreneur, Harold the Headhunter, Martin Luther King, Jr., CEOs of great companies, Sanford Weill, Frederick Smith, Quincy Jones, George Lucas and even for me. It'll work for you in exactly the same way. What results will you get? You'll never know until you try. One thing is certain: "*You get what you want when you give to meet others' needs.*"

Chapter 9
What Has *Become* of Me?

It all starts with a seed. A seed contains within it the potential for life itself. It can grow and become an enormous tree, a beautiful flourishing bush or a colorful flowering plant. However, a seed is not a guarantee of such life. A seed contains only the potential—not a guarantee. A seed can sprout and then wither and die, never reaching its potential. Or worse, a seed that never receives water will simply never germinate or have the opportunity to grow. All of the potential within a seed is just that—potential.

What is most fascinating about how a seed grows is that, at some particular point (when it receives water), life begins to take place. There is a precise point of germination, like a spark that ignites fuel, in which life begins to flow and growth happens. An *ignition point* fuels the growth of that seed. Then, over a period of time, the seed grows *into* something. It becomes more than a seed. It *becomes* what it is created to be—a towering tree, a vibrant flower or fruitful plant.

You are not a seed! But in many ways, your life and what you *become* is much like a seed. You have within you the potential for a great and abundant life—but simply being alive is not a guarantee of such a life. What you *become* in life is determined by your choice to contribute or not to contribute. The choice to contribute is the *ignition point* that fuels growth in your life. The decision to contribute is the precise point in which real life begins to flow and growth takes place. Just like the seed, you will grow *into* something when the ignition point takes place. You will *become* something more.

Unlike the seed, we have a choice. In life we make the choice for ourselves—to contribute and become something more, or to withhold and wither and die. The principles within the *Law of Contribution* hold true—when you are outward focused (contributing), you develop and grow. When you are inward focused (failing to contribute), you wither and die. Let me explain the dynamics that produce these results.

The Seeds of Capacity and Character

When you contribute in life, you ignite the seeds of *capacity* and *character* that are dormant within you. The act of contributing requires that you exercise either (a) a skill or ability or (b) a character trait or virtue.

When you use your skills and abilities in the act of a contribution, you grow the seed of capacity in your life. That capacity is also known as your competence, capability or craft. When you contribute by exercising a character trait or virtue, like love or respect, you grow the seed of character in your life. The act of contributing ignites and fuels the growth of these seeds of capacity and character.

The Seed of Capacity

Work is the primary garden in which your seed of capacity can grow. As Winston Churchill said, "You don't make a living by what you get, you make a living by what you give." When you go to work determined to contribute all you can, you engage all your skills and abilities in the achievement of your task. When you make the choice to do that on a daily basis, you not only discover your real capacity, but you exercise and develop your talents and skills. The more you choose to contribute, the stronger your talent becomes. It's like the act of exercising a muscle in your body. Every day you lift a weight, your muscle becomes stronger.

When it comes to your capabilities, *what* you give is *what* will grow. All people have special capacities—their talents and skills—that lie within them, like the dormant plant within the hard shell of the seed, waiting to come to life. In order to ignite those capabilities, you need to make the choice to contribute. The more you give, the more you exercise and strengthen your resources, further enabling greater and greater contributions.

The Seed of Character

One of the simplest truths is that you cultivate within yourself those things you learn to give. When you give love, you exercise love and in doing so you grow the character of love within yourself. When you *give* love you *become* more loving. When you treat others with kindness and respect you *become* a kind and respectful person. When you are good to other people, you *become* a good person. You cannot own these character traits without first giving them to others. They develop in you and grow like a seed when you ignite them by choosing to give them away. They are exercised and strengthened each and every time you make the choice to use them. The decision to contribute these virtues activates their growth in your life. *What* you give is *what* will grow.

Here is the key principle: ***What you get when you give is not nearly as valuable as what you become when you give. When you give, you don't just get something in return, you become more as a person.*** When you give, *you* grow! When you contribute consistently, over a period of time, the seeds of capacity and character turn you *into* something more. You *become* what you are created to be: a fruitful, contributing and significant person. You become a person of value, and that is what makes you successful.

> *Try not to become a man of success, but rather try to become a man of value.*

> - Einstein

What Prevents These Seeds from Growing?

If contributing produces such wonderful growth results, then why don't we just naturally make those choices more and more? I can give you some suggestions: Because your boss is a greedy, selfish individual and contributing your very best would fill his already bulging bank account. Because the last time you produced your very best work, your manager failed to thank you or even recognize your achievement. Because the last time you really pushed yourself, you fell short of the results you hoped for and were embarrassed that others might see your weakness. Because the last relationship you were in ended painfully and you're not sure it's safe to express love that way again. Because your parents, or teacher or friend told you how hopeless you are. Because you don't believe you have a skill or ability you are good at.

These are but a few of the lies that prevent us from contributing. It's important to recognize that the common element preventing us from contributing is *fear*. We are afraid that if we contribute, someone else will benefit more than us, we won't get a fair return for our efforts, we will be rejected or we will be hurt. Fear drives us to think these thoughts, and fear prevents us from contributing for these reasons. However, what we fail to realize is that by failing to contribute all we can, we fail to *become* the person we can be.

It doesn't make sense to allow fear to control us in this way. When we do, we miss out on everything life has to offer. What's worse is that even if all of these fears did come to pass, the truth remains: "What you *get* when you give is not nearly as valuable as what you *become* when you give." Who cares if your boss won't recognize your achievements? Do it anyway and become so skilled and talented that you can go work anywhere you want. Who cares if your partner rejects your love? Become the most loving person you know and you'll attract any partner you want. By not contributing, you rob yourself of *becoming* something more. Fear is a toothless monster.

I believe that fear is evil. Its objective is to rob us of life. Fear fuels what I call the Spirit of Stillness. This spirit injects our minds with the tranquilizing drug of complacency. It immobilizes us from taking action. As long as we are complacent, as long as we are still, we don't contribute, and we fail to accomplish our purpose. By preventing you from contributing, the Spirit of Stillness prevents growth in your life, because where there is no contribution, there is no growth. The tactic of this spirit is quite simple. As long as you are watching TV, playing video games, hanging out in the bar with your friends—in short, amused by entertainment—there is no opportunity for growth. The antidote for this is *contribution*.

Mackenzie Snyder provides us with a wonderful example of how her decision to contribute ignited the seeds of capacity and character in her life and produced a level of personal growth she could have never expected. The story comes from the book *Chicken Soup for the Preteen Soul*.

In the second grade, Mackenzie and her brothers entered an essay contest that asked the children to identify things they could do to make the world a better place. They won the contest and were chosen to represent the USA at the Children's World Summit. While she was there, Mackenzie met two foster-care kids. As a result, she learned a lot about what foster-care kids go through. They told her that when kids go into the foster-care system, those are the loneliest of times. They don't just lose their parents and home; they are also often separated from their brothers and sisters. They told her that when the kids are picked up from their home by a social worker, they are given only a trash bag to put their few belongings into. This trash bag is what foster-care kids carry with them when they are moved from home to home.

Deeply saddened when she heard this, Mackenzie wondered what it would be like to have to live out of a trash bag. She made the decision that she wanted to help foster-care kids. She said, "These kids needed my help, because they were not being respected like they should be."

At the age of seven, she made the decision to contribute and began her own project for foster-care kids. She decided she would do something practical to help these unfortunate children.

She started by asking her mom to stop at garage sales when she saw suitcases or duffle bags for sale. She explained to the people selling the bags that she wanted to use them to help foster-care kids, and frequently they gave her the bags free. She said, "I tried to put myself into the mind of a foster-care kid, and I decided that the kids should have a stuffed animal in the bag too. I figured if I was in that situation, I would want a cuddly friend to hug when I was sad and felt lonely for my parents." People gave her those free, too.

In October of 1998, Mackenzie helped organize a luggage drive during their local community "Make a Difference Day." Some members of the Congress and Senate showed up and noted her project. They went back to Washington and told others about what Mackenzie was doing. As a result, she received a $15,000 grant, which attracted media attention and a cover story in the *Washington Post*. Next, the president of the United States read about her initiative in the *Washington Post* and wanted to meet with her. Imagine that! After meeting the president and first lady, she said, "They were so nice, and I gave the President one of my bags with a Beanie Baby in it to give to any foster-kid that he may meet. A few days later, he sent some bags to me from his own collection to give to foster-care kids, so I did."

Her project grew rapidly as a result of all the media attention. Radio stations called and she even made an appearance on the *Rosie O'Donnell Show*. She said that several thousand bags had already been sent out and she had 5,000 more ready to go. Each bag contained a luggage tag designed by her. In each bag she puts a cuddly stuffed animal and a special note written by her:

Dear friend,

Hi, my name is Mackenzie Snyder. I am nine years old, and I am in third grade. I collect suitcases and duffle bags as an act of kindness for those who are in need of them. God told me you could use a duffle bag and a cuddly friend so I sent this with love to you. I want you to always know that you are loved, especially by me. And always remember to be positive, polite and never give up.

Love, your friend,
Mackenzie Snyder

She says, "There are 530,000 foster-care kids in the United States. My dream is for all the foster-care kids in the entire United States to receive a duffle bag and a cuddly friend. It is a lot of work but I never get tired of it."[43]

Don't let the tears in your eyes prevent you from seeing what really happened here. First of all, Mackenzie did something by the age of nine that few people do by the age of sixty—she touched her potential. It was her *decision* to contribute that ignited the growth and development of both her capacity and her character.

First of all, her capacity—that is, her skills, abilities and level of competence—grew when she began contributing. Her project required ingenuity. She not only found a way to obtain duffle bags and stuffed animals, but also to convince people to give them to her for free. Her project also required a great deal of organization. At the time of the writing of her story, she reported having 5,000 duffle bags, each containing a stuffed animal, her luggage tag and a letter, all sitting in her house! She also demonstrated a great deal of initiative. Her goal is to continue until she reaches all of the foster-care kids in the USA. I wonder how many companies in North America would be willing to pay top wages to employees who had the *capacity* of this nine year old?

In the same way, her character grew when she began contributing. There is no doubt that this little girl had a great deal of character before she even started this project. However, the more love, kindness and respect she showed by her acts of contribution, the more her character came into full bloom. Clearly, her life will never be the same. The *act* of contributing made an impact on her life that she could not have experienced by simply writing about, talking about or wishing she could do something to help. When we make the decision to contribute, the seeds of capacity and character ignite, come to life and grow.

The final point of this story is the most important. What Mackenzie *became* in the process of contributing was what Einstein referred to as a "person of value." While many nine year olds spend their time watching TV, numbed by stillness, this little girl defined a life of *value*, all because of a choice to contribute.

Every day, we have the option to choose to contribute or not. Every day is an opportunity to ignite, nurture and grow our seeds of capacity and character. Opportunities for contribution take place everywhere—at home, with friends, with strangers and at work. We realize our potential only when we embrace each opportunity to contribute. Although these kinds of stories are nice, contributing in real life is not always easy. I know that from personal experience. Yet I have found that the more I give when I am tested, the more I grow in the process.

Growth Can Be Both Slow and Painful

I am a slow learner. I have been observing the *Law of Contribution* for about 15 years, and learning even more about it as I wrote this book over the past four years. Even so, only a few years ago, I was still having a hard time applying the principle in everyday life.

Several years ago, I took a position with a company as a consultant. I wasn't excited about the job, but I needed the work, and this opportunity presented itself, so there I was. (Perhaps that predicament was, in itself, enough to suggest that I had a lot to learn about contributing.)

Inspired by what I was learning about the impact of contributing, I made the commitment that I would approach this project with the attitude that I would contribute everything I had to give, my full effort, regardless of the situation. The decision at the time seemed like a simple one. Little did I know how difficult a test of faith it would become.

Initially, I learned about the company, its market and the opportunity for growth that seemed obvious to me. Although this was beyond the requirements of my role, I took the owners of the company aside and presented my findings to them. They liked what I had to say and asked for a more detailed plan. I poured myself into the request and presented them with the best work I had ever prepared. I discovered a skill I had not previously had the opportunity to use.

The presentation and implementation of the plan was an enormous success. It changed the direction of the company and more than doubled its sales in the first year of implementation.

Because the plan was my own, I had the opportunity to participate in its implementation in that first year, which allowed me to discover and use new skills. My decision to contribute had ignited my capacity, and I was growing.

However, my character was in for a bit of a jolt. Although everything I had proposed had been working out perfectly for the company, the CEO was not always appreciative of my contributions. At times, when I felt I was working in the best interest of the company, the CEO would misinterpret my actions and attack me—sometimes doing so openly for others to see.

As time passed, he learned that my intentions were valid and accepted them; however, at the time I was furious. "After all I did for him," I thought, "look at how he treats me!" Maintaining my commitment to contribute was a true test of my character. If I had not made the decision to continue contributing, my seed of character would have withered and died, and I would have missed a key opportunity for growth. Somehow, I made the right decision.

As time passed, I continued to contribute by expanding my original plan, which resulted in extraordinary growth for the company. As a direct result of my initiatives, revenues grew by 400 percent in four years. The company received several awards for national growth. Did I receive the kind of reward or recognition I deserved? I don't know, but it doesn't matter. With an outward-focused mindset, I grew to understand the person I reported to and gained a great amount of respect for him. I am grateful for the opportunity to have worked with him.

In the end, what was most important was that my capacity—my skills and abilities—grew to new heights. The experience I gained in that role helped me form my own consulting firm. Most of all, my character grew into something more than it was when I started. I had learned that *what you get when you give is not nearly as valuable as what you become when you give.*

All of this had taken place over a period of years. Often, this is how growth takes place—slowly. At this very moment, the hairs on your head are growing (even if you don't have much hair). You can't feel it happening, and if you look in the mirror, you won't be able to see it happening either. However, just because you can't feel or see it, doesn't mean growth is not taking place. In time, that growth becomes obvious. One day, you look in the mirror and realize, "My hair is getting long; I need a haircut."

The process of personal growth and development is much the same. When you contribute in life, you exercise your skills, abilities and greater values, which cause you to grow each and every day—little by little. Each decision you make to contribute, big or small, is an action that fuels growth in your life. Those decisions cause you to grow, a bit at a time—much like the hair on your head. After some time, you grow into something more. You become what you were created to be. One day, you look in the mirror and realize, "Hey, I'm not a seed! I'm a towering tree, a vibrant flower, a fruitful plant. I have become what I am created to be. I have capacity, I have character, and I am proud of what I have *become*."

Chapter 10
Don't Die Without It!

Harold Kushner, in his book *Living a Life That Matters*, describes how he has been with many people on their deathbed, most of whom are not afraid of dying. What he has noticed, however, is that the people who had the most trouble with death were those who felt they had never done anything worthwhile with their lives. It was not death that frightened them—it was insignificance. We all want to feel like our lives had some kind of meaning—that we mattered or made a difference. Perhaps our greatest fear of all is the fear that our life did not matter.

Our fear as adults is not that much different than the fear of our children on Easter morning. With her eyes wide with anticipation, the child lifts the chocolate bunny and bites into one of the long ears. The child looks at the candy in her hand. Just what she feared: it's hollow! The fear we have about our lives is the same. We don't ever want to get to a point where we feel that our life is hollow. Every one of us craves a life of substance, a life that matters.

The only road that leads to a life of purpose and fulfillment is the one filled with contributions to others. The *Law of Contribution* is based on the idea that our whole life is wrapped up in the one universal truth that we are made to look out for each other. It's a kind of code for human conduct. When we violate this natural law in the way we live, our hearts struggle with the haunting feeling of insignificance. If we ever find ourselves feeling "empty" or feeling like we have "nothing to live for," it's the natural result of a life that is focused on self rather than others. Somewhere, we've made a wrong turn on the road.

A life focused primarily on self-success, self-gratification and self-satisfaction is not a life of substance. When contribution is missing, so is the sense of purpose and fulfillment. We can learn from those who have been down that road.

Dexter Manley had success, but purpose and fulfillment eluded him. He played in three Super Bowls, winning twice. Known as the "Secretary of Defense," the six-foot-three, 260-pound NFL defensive end compiled an impressive 97 sacks during his career.

Growing up in the projects of Houston, Manley was given an athletic scholarship to Oklahoma State University, despite his inability to read or write. After a stellar college football career, Manley was drafted into the National Football League. For nine seasons, from 1981 to 1989, he played for the Washington Redskins. A former teammate said he was "…as physically gifted a football player as I've seen."[44]

But as hard as Manley played, he partied even harder. He indulged in all the things he wanted: expensive clothes, extravagant living, cars and eventually, drugs. His life became a pursuit of personal gratification.

By the middle of the 1980s, the star was abusing cocaine. In 1991, the NFL banned him from the league. After two lackluster seasons in Canada's football league, his playing days came to an end. Yet Manley continued to live as if he was still a player. He carried his expired NFL Players Association card for identification. He stayed in Marriott hotels, just as he did when he was with the Red-skins. Questioned about his profession, he'd reply, "football player." Manley continued doing drugs as well and, in 2002, he received a two-year prison sentence for cocaine possession.

In an interview with the *New York Times*, Manley said, "Once it was over [playing football], I had nothing to live for."[45] Having lived only for himself, he failed to contribute, and was forced to acknowledge that his life was "hollow." A life without contribution is a life without purpose and fulfillment.

Don Hewitt, the executive producer of *60 Minutes* explained that at the age of 81—nearing the end of his life—he too reached that difficult place in the road. Having retired from his long-running and successful television program, Hewitt should have been content to bask in the glow of his success. He had received multiple Emmy Awards and his life was full of memories of encounters with celebrities, presidents and kings. But by Hewitt's own admission, he said he felt "empty." One article recounts Hewitt's frustrations:

> Hewitt strode into his office and gestured toward the walls. There hung photographs of presidents, diplomats, foreign leaders and entertainers. There were notes from Presidents Reagan and Eisenhower. A constellation of Emmy Awards. Arrays of plaques, posters and medallions. Then, in the midst of all of this he admitted that these things did not bring the substance we all crave. Looking for that sense of purpose, he said, "What I've got to do is feed my soul."[46]

Our soul is fed and our life contains purpose and fulfillment when we live to serve, to help and to contribute. This issue that both Manley and Hewitt admit to is what all of us fear—reaching a point where we realize our life is hollow. The common downfall of such people is that they fail to live beyond self-success, self-gratification and self-satisfaction. Innately, we want more. We want to feel fulfilled. And that can only come when our lives contain contribution.

All people of substance have recognized that serving, contributing, helping and promoting goodness is the underlying attitude that supports a purposeful life.

The purpose of human life is to serve, and to show compassion and the will to help others.

- Albert Schweitzer

Life finds its purpose and fulfillment in the expansion of happiness.

- Maharishi Mahesh Yogi

Contributing in life and helping others is the common thread in the lives of people who have purpose and fulfillment. Consider the example of San Antonio Spurs basketball star David Robinson. He is an original Dream Teamer, an MVP, a Rookie of the Year, a Defensive Player of the Year, a scoring champion, a ten-time all star and a sure-fire bet for induction into the Basketball Hall of Fame. However, his life is significant because of the accomplishments he has made off the court and how he contributes with his life. He uses what he has—his money and influence—for more than his own self-satisfaction and glory. His reputation within his hometown of San Antonio, Texas, follows him.

The *Boston Globe* reports, "You cannot imagine how this city and its citizens adore the retiring Spurs center." Assistant coach P. J. Carlesimo states, "*Revere* is not too strong a word to describe the way they feel about him."[47]

His latest project is the Carver Academy, a faith-based private school for kids from the inner city; most of them are Hispanic and African American. Robinson has donated more than $9 million to get the school off the ground and takes a personal interest in the kids.

Coach Gregg Popovich doubts he'll see much of Robinson hanging around the locker room or seeking a job in the front office:

> *He's got much more sense than to stay involved in basketball. He's got interests that actually have impact on the world and have some value, unlike the rest of us. I wouldn't demean him by approaching him with [an offer to work for the Spurs].... I think he's way too committed to do something as silly as basketball the rest of his life.*[48]

Robinson has chosen to contribute to the needs of others and, in doing so, is making an impact on his world. Manley could have done the same with a decision to contribute beyond himself. When we look at the lives of people with substance, we see a common thread—their lives are focused on more than their own self-satisfaction. They approach life with an attitude of contribution and a desire to help those around them. A purpose-filled life is a life that contains an attitude of service.

> *I desire to leave to the men that come after me a remembrance of me in good works.*

- Alfred the Great

Serving others seems to bring greater fulfillment than serving self. There are people who have "had it all" and recognized early enough that they wanted more from life. Willing to make a sacrifice, they are not the kind of people who are forced to use words like "empty" and "nothing to live for" to describe their life. Instead, they say, "I was born to do this work," or "I wouldn't trade this for anything in the world."

Susie Scott Krabacher is one such person. For her, having it all was becoming "Miss May, 1983" in *Playboy* magazine and spending time at Hugh Hefner's mansion. Yet she began looking for a purpose for her life. At the urging of a friend, she made a trip to Haiti. From that initial visit came the determination to devote her life to helping Haitian children.

The Haitians did not take the blonde American beauty seriously—at first. "They thought I'd pass out candy and toys, make promises, get my name in the paper, and go home as soon as I got scared,"[49] she says. But through her commitment to serve, she has made an enormous impact on that part of the world. Her nonprofit foundation has raised millions of dollars and used the money to build six schools, three orphanages and a hospital. She went from "Playmate" to the name that hundreds of Haitian children now call her: "Mama."

Does such sacrifice bring purpose and meaning? "I was born to do this work," says Krabacher. "I was not put here to be a *Playboy* centerfold." How many people do you know who can say, "I was born to do this work"?

The only way life rewards us with a sense of purpose and fulfillment is when we begin to reach out to others. When we finally learn to cooperate with the *Law of Contribution*, we feel a whole different way about life. This is not the path society promotes. But it is the path many have taken.

Teach this triple truth to all: A generous heart, kind speech, and a life of service and compassion are the things that renew humanity.

- Buddha

Mary Brenner is another example of a person who chose to exchange what many would call a glamorous life for a life of service to others. Mary was raised in Beverly Hills, where she lived what she called "a glamorous life," until she decided there was more to life than serving herself. Now, the small American woman in her 70s is known as Sister Antonia to the inmates and guards at La Mesa Prison in Tijuana, Mexico. She lives in a sparse ten-foot cell inside the prison. She moved there 25 years ago to live among murderers, thieves and drug dealers. Sister Antonia has poured out her life for these prisoners, nursing their wounds, getting them eyeglasses and medicine, caring for their families, and washing their bodies for burial. She refers to each prisoner as her son.

Although she lives in a prison, the prison does not live inside her. Her friends and the inmates all describe her incredible energy, joy and hopefulness. She describes it as simply living out her calling. In a recent interview, she said, "I wouldn't trade this cell for any place in the world."

I don't know what your destiny will be, but one thing I do know: the only ones among you who will be really happy are those who have sought and found how to serve.

- Albert Schweitzer

A life focused on serving and contributing is filled with purpose and meaning—even when the external luxuries are gone. The examples of Sister Antonia and Mama demonstrate that serving others can be remarkably rewarding, even though they sacrificed what many would not. How many people do you know who can say, "I was made for this," or "I would not trade this for anything in the world"? They can.

In case you're getting nervous, you do not need to move to a third-world country to feed the poor or surrender your life to a jail cell in order to serve others and have a purposeful or meaningful life. What is significant to note, however, is that even in those harsh conditions, life can be fulfilling when you are contributing. Clearly, contributing is the foundation of a purposeful life.

Where Do I Start?

At this point, you may think a life of contribution means completely ignoring your own needs, desires and goals and focusing your life entirely on service to others. This is not the case. Learning to contribute in life starts with an *attitude*. When our attitude is one that desires to contribute to others, we will discover opportunities to serve and make a difference. In every case, those opportunities are already present in your life. An outward-focused view simply helps you see them.

All you need to do to find opportunities to contribute is look around "your world." Your world is different than my world. The people you will have the potential to contact are different than the people I will, than your spouse will, or than your kids will. We each may have overlapping contacts, but our precise circle of influence in the world is unique. Your daily interactions with others contain within them opportunities for contribution that only you have. There are often opportunities that only you can "see." We can learn to see and seize these opportunities when we approach life with an outward attitude and a desire to contribute.

We start the journey toward a purposeful and fulfilling life with a single act of kindness. We find opportunities to meet others' needs when we are sensitive to others' needs. In the book *Random Acts of Kindness*, Abby tells the story of how someone did that for her.

Abby explains that she had just broken up from a long and painful relationship and found herself in a new city without friends, without anything to do and without the desire to do anything. Every day, she would come home from work and just stare at the walls, sometimes crying, but mostly just sitting and wondering if this cloud would ever go away.

She had bought an answering machine, which she admits she had no use for. She didn't know anybody, and no one ever called her. But one night, she came home and the red light was flashing. When she played it back, she said, "A wonderful male voice started to apologize that he had called the wrong number. But then he kept talking." He said her voice on the message sounded so sad and that he just wanted to tell her it was okay to be sad, that being able to feel that sadness was important. He went on for almost twenty minutes talking about how important it was to be able to go through the pain instead of running away from it, and how even though it might seem impossible now, things would get better. She finished the story by saying, "He never said his name, but that message was, in a very important way, the beginning of my life."

In this example, the man who left the message was obviously sensitive to what he heard on the answering machine. He recognized the need (a sad person) that he could help in a very simple, but profound way. We can find opportunities to contribute when we look for them.

You will discover a greater purpose for your life when you look for opportunities to contribute. The key is that you must *start* by contributing. A greater purpose and cause often unfolds in the lives of people who contribute and look for ways to help and serve. This is what happened to Henri Durant. He saw a need and started a movement that today has saved millions of people.

Henri Durant was a wealthy nineteenth-century Swiss banker. He was sent to Paris by the Swiss government to work on a business deal with Napoleon. He arrived only to be informed that Napoleon was off fighting a war against the Austrians in Solferino, Italy. So Durant got back into his carriage and sent his horses galloping down to the battlefront. He got there just in time to hear the bugles blast and see the thundering charge of Napoleon's troops. Durant had never before witnessed the ghastly carnage of war. He watched in horror as cannonballs tore through human flesh, and acres of land became heaped with maimed and dying men. Henri Durant was so devastated that he remained at the front for weeks helping doctors tend to the wounded in churches and nearby farmhouses.

After his return to Switzerland, Durant continued to be haunted by the images of war he had seen in Italy. He could not keep his mind on banking, becoming so distracted that he lost his fortune.

Out of his depression and failure—after following the wrong road to Italy—Henri Durant founded the Red Cross, which has saved millions of lives and given aid to countless victims of war and disaster over the years. For establishing this organization, he received the first Nobel Peace Prize. It was because Durant had an outward focus that he was able to "see" a desperate need and start the Red Cross.

It's that same outward focus that helped nine-year-old Mackenzie "see" foster-children's need. It's that same outward focus that helped David Robinson "see" the needs of those in San Antonio. It's that same outward focus that helped the man who dialed a wrong phone number "see" the need in the voice of a lonely young woman.

> *What do we live for if it is not to make life less difficult for each other?*
>
> - George Elliot

When you look for opportunities to contribute, you'll "see" them. If you stop focusing on yourself for just a brief moment and stop to look around to consider the needs of those around you, you will be shocked at exactly how much need you will "see." A purposeful and fulfilling life starts with your willingness to see and serve the needs of others. You start by contributing to those in your world in whatever ways present themselves. You start where you are, with what you have.

If you are a journalist, you can begin by writing about the needs of people in "your world." Rather than exposing crime, you can expose needs, issues, and cries for help. If you are a business owner, you can use your influence and financial resources to reach out to those in your world. If you are a pastor of a church, you can inspire your congregation to do more than show up for church on Sunday; you can inspire them to show up where your community has real needs. And, if you are the manager of a local grocery store, you can do what Tony has been doing for the past 20 years.

Tony was a gentle, self-effacing manager of a small-town supermarket who never stopped helping people. Whether it was carrying out your groceries on a stormy winter day, helping people pay for their groceries when they were short, or sending food to someone he knew had a need, Tony was decent, generous and kind. Among the local residents, almost everybody had at least one story about Tony's outward-focused acts.

Few people fully appreciated what Tony meant to the small community, until he was assigned to another store. The residents could not believe it. Word spread quickly. Neighbors called each other in shock: "Tony's gone." Some plotted strategies for bringing Tony back and staged protest marches outside the store. Others flooded the local newspaper with angry letters. The mayor took up the cause. Even the police tried to set things right.

A grocer seems an unlikely figure to set off such an emotional outpouring. The fact that he did shows the remarkable effect Tony—a man of endless warmth and good humor—had on people.

The local police said no one was more helpful. "We'd often have kids who needed a job—not honor students, kids in trouble, who'd been before the judge—and Tony would hire them every time. Nine times out of ten, it probably wouldn't work out, but he never hesitated."

The local pastor agreed: "He was always willing to take risks on people. He used to say to me, 'You and I are in the same business—the people business.'"

Tony confirmed that he didn't see his purpose as one of selling groceries, but as one of helping people. He said, "You're selling groceries, but what really matters is your relationships with people." What Tony saw were needs, and he made every day an opportunity for contribution.

Purposeful living is contributing to those in your world, with what you have, where you are. It's choosing, like Tony did, to see what you do every day as an opportunity to contribute. I don't believe that one day you just *discover* your purpose. Rather, your life becomes *full* of purpose when you look for and begin to find ways to contribute. From those contributions comes a greater cause and purpose for life.

In the end, a life of purpose is really quite simple. It's a life that asks, "How can I serve? How can I help? What can I contribute?" Don't die without answering that question!

Chapter 11
This Really Does *Feel* Good

Did you know that how you feel physically and mentally may be directly related to how inward or outward focused you are? It's true. In fact, your focus may even have an impact on how long you live! When you perform an outward-focused act, or even think an outward-focused thought, there is a response in your body that triggers a host of physiological benefits, including immediate good feelings, improved emotional well being, reduction in physical illness, improved immune system functioning and even extended life expectancy. When you are outward focused, it's as if your body says, "This is good for you!"

When you carry out acts of kindness you get a wonderful feeling inside. It is as though something inside your body responds and says, "Yes, this is how I ought to feel."

- Rabbi Harold Kushner

Likewise, when you are inward focused, your body triggers emotions that are destructive, which serve to make you feel lousy, depress your immune system and even shorten your life. When you are inward focused, it's as if your body says, "This is not good for you—stop!"

Heeding the *Law of Contribution* may help improve both your health and the number of positive emotions and good feelings you experience in life. The evidence seems to suggest that living with an outward focus is part of our innate design as humans—causing you to reap all kinds of physical and mental benefits when you serve others.

At first glance, outward-focused acts seem to require true sacrifice, whereby you temporarily set aside yourself in consideration for someone else. It appears that you must choose the needs of another over your own. However, upon closer examination, this sacrifice actually offers more benefits to the giver than the receiver. It is literally true that serving others may in fact be one of the most self-serving things you can do.

What's Really Going On?

The Institute of HeartMath,® a nonprofit research and education organization, has conducted research that helps identify what's going on in our body when we experience positive emotions like the ones produced by an outward focus, and negative emotions like the ones produced by an inward focus.

Over the years, they experimented with different psychological and physiological measures, but heart rate variability, or heart rhythms, stood out as the most consistent reflection of inner emotional states. It became clear that positive emotions create increased harmony and coherence in heart rhythms and improved balance in the nervous system. In contrast, negative emotions lead to disorder in the heart's rhythms and autonomic nervous system, adversely affecting the rest of the body. The health implications are easy to understand: disharmony in the nervous system is stressful to the heart and other organs, while harmony is less stressful to the body's systems.

Heart Rhythms and Your "Focus"

When you experience positive emotions, like those created by an outward focus—appreciation, care, joy or love—your heart rhythm pattern becomes more ordered and coherent (see Figure 1).

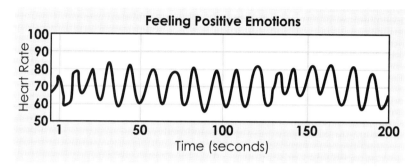

Figure 1: Heart rhythms when experiencing positive emotions

When you experience negative emotions, like those created by an inward-focus—tension, anxiety, irritation or anger—your heart rhythm pattern becomes irregular and incoherent, which negatively affects health, brain function, performance and your sense of well-being (see Figure 2).

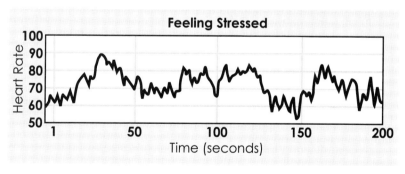

Figure 2: Heart rhythms when experiencing negative emotions

While this might sound like a lot of jargon, it means you feel good—mentally and physically—when you are outward focused, and this feel-good sensation has a direct effect on your overall health.

Research conducted by Allan Luks and Peggy Payne reported in the book *The Healing Power of Doing Good* confirms this.

The research demonstrates that outward-focused actions, specifically, helping others, produces both an immediate, short-term "feel-good" benefit and an extended, long-term health benefit. According to the research conducted by Luks and Payne, the act of helping others produces a two-fold effect in which the giver experiences two specific stages of physiological benefits.

The first phase is what Luks and Payne call the Helper's High. This is the sensation that follows immediately after performing an outward act. It begins with a physical high. Helpers get an immediate feel-good sensation—a rush of good feelings. They often report feeling sudden warmth, increased energy and even a sense of euphoria. A total of 95 percent of the volunteers in their survey reported this physical feel-good sensation: 54 percent reported warmth, 29 percent reported increased energy, and 21 percent reported drug-like euphoria. This Helper's High involves physical sensations that strongly indicate a sharp reduction in stress and the release of the body's natural pain killers: the endorphins.[50]

The second phase is what Luks and Payne call the Healthy Helping Syndrome.

The initial Helper's High rush is followed by this syndrome—a longer-lasting period of improved emotional well-being. Helpers report a sense of calmness, feelings of increased self-worth and relaxation. Specifically, 57 percent mentioned an increase in self-worth and 53 percent mentioned greater happiness and optimism and fewer feelings of helplessness and depression. Some of the tangible health benefits reported included the reduction of headaches and back pain, improved sleep and reduced arthritis pain and the like.[51]

As an example, one of the volunteers reported the following: "…when I am helping someone I feel the best. When I was in college, I would get really stressed out and get bad headaches. As soon as I would volunteer somewhere, my headaches would stop, my energy would improve. I would do fantastically on my tests, and I enjoyed even dreary tasks more."[52]

These physical sensations are indicators of improved health. Studies show that your immune system is strengthened when you perform outward acts. No pills required. One of the studies confirming this is found in the research paper "The Physiological and Psychological Effects of Compassion and Anger."[53]

In this study, individuals were instructed to arouse certain emotional states. One group was to arouse positive emotions of care and compassion—like those produced by outward-focused thoughts—and the other group was to arouse negative emotions of anger and frustration—like those produced by inward-focused thoughts. Immune system function (salivary IgA, or S-IgA), heart rate and mood were measured in the test subjects before and after experiencing the emotional states of care and compassion and anger and frustration.

The test results demonstrated that positive emotions produce remarkable health benefits. Test subjects who experienced the positive emotions of care and compassion had a tendency toward *increased* levels of immune system function over the following six hours. Conversely, test subjects who experienced anger and frustration showed a large *decrease* in immune system function for an additional five hours.

Additionally, the care and compassion group experienced dramatic decreases in tension-anxiety, anger-hostility, fatigue and confusion as well as an increase in vigor. The anger and frustration group, on the other hand, experienced the exact opposite. They reported a variety of physical symptoms, including headaches, indigestion, muscle pains and fatigue. The only physical symptom reported by the care and compassion group was that of relaxation.

One of the main findings from this study is the revelation that a simple five-minute period of experiencing care and compassion immediately produced a significant increase in immune system function (S-IgA levels), while experiencing five minutes of anger and frustration did not.

A similar, quite famous study produced the same result, calling it the Mother Teresa Effect. David McClelland at Harvard led the study. Researchers instructed 132 students to watch a 50-minute film about Mother Teresa aiding the sick and dying of Calcutta. After the film, they tested a sample of saliva from each participant and found that the students who had seen the film showed marked increases in their immune system function.[54] Our body seems to automatically produce a kind of life-giving energy when exposed to outward-focused actions.

Why is the immune system important? Bacteria, viruses and other microorganisms must first penetrate our immune system's defenses. This defense system is enhanced and buffered by positive emotions produced by outward thoughts and actions. The stronger your immune system, the less likely you will become sick or experience disease. And the less disease you have, the longer you live, which is another minor benefit of outward-focused actions. Many studies prove this to be true.

Researchers at the University of Michigan recently discovered that the survival rate of seniors who volunteered 40 or more hours a year for a single cause was 40 percent greater than that of non-volunteers.[55]

Stephanie Brown, evolutionary psychologist at the University of Michigan, also studied elderly people involved in giving. Her study profiled 423 elderly couples for five years. She found that people who provided no help, either practical or emotional, were more than twice as likely to die as their altruistic peers.[56]

The results of other studies on altruism's effect on mortality are similar. In a study of 2,700 residents of Tecumseh, Michigan, researchers found that men who volunteered in their community were two and a half times less likely to die than non-volunteering men.[57]

All the Benefits of Meditation

Herbert Benson, M.D., author of *The Relaxation Response* and *The Breakout Principle*, sees helping others as producing the same benefits as meditation. He states, "The key, in helping as in meditation, whether you're repeating a mantra or teaching an illiterate how to read, is that you're concentrating on a point outside of yourself. What happens physically is that the out-of-self focus breaks into the person's usual tension-producing thought patterns, decreasing the activity of the sympathetic nervous system and thereby countermanding the body's stress reactions."[58] An outward focus requires the same mental outlook as meditation and produces similar benefits.

Other researchers have also discovered the benefits of focusing beyond self. Researcher Carolyn Schwartz, Sc.D., of the University of Massachusetts Medical School, says, "The act of giving to someone else may have mental-health benefits because the very nature of focusing outside the self counters the self-focused nature of anxiety or depression."[59]

An outward focus also serves as a natural remedy for depression. The power helping others has on mental health is widely recognized by many health professionals. Irvin Yalom, M.D., author of *The Theory and Practice of Group Psychotherapy*, says, "Psychiatric patients beginning therapy are demoralized and possess a deep sense of having nothing of value to offer others." In other words, they do not believe they have anything to contribute. Yalom says, "The experience of finding they can be of importance to others is refreshing and boosts self-esteem."[60] When people who are depressed learn to have outward thoughts and take outward actions, they begin to get well. As Allan Luks notes,

> *Almost any volunteer will tell you that helping somebody else is good for curing a case of the blues. More than that, for many people helping others has been the agent that has made it possible to get through major life crises, to end bouts of depression that grow out of tremendous losses. Some argue that a couple of hours at work as a helper are as good as a strong antidepressant.*[61]

My friend Mary was suffering from a mild case of depression. She was depressed because, in her words, "life has little meaning." She felt that there was little in her life worth living for. However, because depression was new to her, she immediately went to the doctor to obtain antidepressant medication. When I heard about this, I became concerned. I began going to church with Mary, and we found that there was an opportunity for her to perform volunteer work with special needs children. Helping special needs kids was something Mary had always wanted to do. Every Sunday morning, Mary began going to church to help others in this way. She and the children soon began to build friendships and special bonds. She even began helping the kids in others ways, beyond Sunday mornings. She loved it. Her contribution was having a real and positive impact on the lives of others. Mary began to recognize that what she did mattered. Within a few weeks, she had completely forgotten about her previous feelings of depression. In her case, contribution worked significantly faster than any medication and without any negative side effects.

Contribution helps reverse the effects of depression by forcing you to take your mind off yourself. In other words, it helps reverse the "over-concern" with self caused by an inward focus. When you focus on others and what they need, your mind is no longer focused on your own self-perceived problems. An outward focus helps interrupt depressive thinking styles that are driven by too much introspection and rumination.

When you perform outward acts, your body heals itself, both physically and mentally. The following quotation from one of Allan Luks's test subjects is representative of how people benefit from helping others:

Some months ago, I was so stressed out that I could barely get four hours sleep at night and I had all sorts of aches and pains. I had even tried antidepressant and anxiety drugs, but to no avail. I then found out firsthand that it is love that truly heals. When I do nice things, I definitely feel a physical response. For me it is mostly a relaxation of muscles that I hadn't even realized had been tensed...I can now sleep well at night, and most of my aches and pains have disappeared.[62]

Such reports suggest that your body produces the medication you need when you begin contributing. You can take a pill to help alter your mood, or you can do something for someone else. Faced with the evidence that our emotional health improves when we contribute, the decision to contribute seems to be a good one.

If you suffer from depression, consider how you might be able to contribute to the lives of others. The result will benefit not only you, but will make a significant impact on the lives of those you choose to help. The cure lies in learning to become outward focused—in learning to live a life of contribution. The hope you need rests within you. When you begin giving, you begin living.

The Painful Effects of an Inward-focused Life

Just as there are physical and emotional benefits derived from an outward focus, there are equally destructive results produced from an inward focus. The direct correlation between an inward focus and its impact on your health is demonstrated by a research team at the University of California at San Francisco Medical School. They counted the number of times test subjects used words such as "I" and "me" and then correlated these with measures of anger intensity and blood pressure. They found that "Type A" students used twice as many self-references as the "Type B" students, and that self-references were highly correlated with both anger intensity and high blood pressure.[63]

An even stronger correlation was found when the test was repeated with middle-aged men who had been referred by cardiologists for an exercise stress test. The men whose stress tests were abnormal were also likely to rate very high on their "I/me" usage. In addition, the most self-involved patients tended to have more severe cases of coronary artery disease, as well as greater likelihood of depression and anxiety.

An exaggerated focus on self is unhealthy. Negative emotions produced by an inward focus, such as hostility and anger, can suppress your immune system. A study conducted by Dr. Janice Kiecolt-Glaser and Dr. Ronald Glaser confirms this. Ninety newlywed couples were admitted to a hospital research unit for 24 hours. Those who exhibited negative or hostile behaviors during a 30-minute discussion of marital problems showed a less effective immune system for the following 24 hours than those who were more positive and hospitable.[64]

In a separate study, "those who scored in the upper 20 percent of hostility when tested 20 years earlier had a 42 percent increased risk of premature death from all causes combined, including heart disease and cancer, when compared to those who scored in the lower 20 percent of hostility."[65]

In chapter five, we talked about how inward-focused actions are human repellants, driving people away from us. Because of this, people who are inward focused have fewer relationships and tend to be more isolated from others. Besides being a terrible way to live, studies show that being isolated does not bode well for your health either.

In the Alameda County Study, those who lacked social ties were at increased risk of dying from coronary heart disease, stroke, cancer, respiratory diseases, gastrointestinal diseases and all other causes of death. Women who were socially isolated or who just felt they were isolated had a significantly elevated risk of dying of cancer. Similarly, men with few social ties showed significantly poorer cancer survival rates.[66]

In yet another study in Sweden, more than 1,700 men and women between the ages of 29 and 74 were followed for six years. Those who were most lonely and isolated had four times the risk of dying prematurely during this period.[67]

The link between social isolation and mortality is made obvious by researchers in the Beta-Blocker Heart Attack Trial. In this study, they interviewed more than 2,300 men who had survived a heart attack. Those who were classified as being "socially isolated" and having a high degree of life stress had more than four times the risk of death as men who had low levels of both stress and isolation.[68]

By now, the evidence should seem clear. Living with an inward focus offers you nothing in the way of satisfaction in life. In addition, you are more likely to feel lousy, get sick more frequently and even die sooner than if you live with an outward focus. I don't know about you, but the results produced by an inward-focused lifestyle are not what I'm looking for.

On the other hand, the life I want—and I suspect the life you want—is the life that contains all the benefits derived from living with an outward focus—feeling good about yourself, enjoying improved health and even living longer. I want to live longer while feeling good and enjoying life. An outward focus seems to offer that hope.

When it comes to deciding how to get what I want in life, living with an outward focus seems to be a "no-brainer." The physical and mental benefits are too great to ignore. In the next chapter, we'll explore the possibility that the benefits may even extend beyond the physical realm.

Chapter 12
Who's Keeping Score?

Statistically, a high percentage of you reading this book believe there is a universal God who "sees all." Now, while I say that, there will be a small percentage of you who will object to any discussion on the subject of spirituality or any dialogue even containing the "G" word. For this reason, I almost did not include this chapter in this book, fearing that some people might feel that the *Law of Contribution* is not based on solid truths. However, after careful study and consideration, I discovered that *not* including this chapter would make discussion of the law less than complete.

If the *Law of Contribution* really does affect every aspect of our life, then the spiritual realm must also be examined. I found there is substantial evidence that suggests most people believe in a spiritual realm and that it has an important impact on our lives.

What Do People Really Believe about God?

Wherever you are right now, stop and look around. At this very moment, there are radio signals passing through the air transmitting music, words and news. While that might sound strange, because you cannot *see* the data in the air around you, all you need to do is turn on the radio to prove this is true. In the same way, there are thousands, probably millions, of cellular telephone conversations taking place right now, whereby voice signals are being transmitted invisibly through the air via cellular towers, yet you cannot *see* these either. Does that mean they are not real and do not exist? Of course not. We all know they exist although we cannot see them.

Likewise, there seems to be a common belief among humans that although we cannot see a spiritual realm, we believe it exists. Statistics show that 96 percent of people believe there is a God. Chances are high that you believe this too. Since God is a spiritual being we cannot see, but must have faith to believe in, it appears as though people have an innate certainty in a greater spiritual realm. Although we might struggle with what this means, and we might argue about various spiritual beliefs, we do seem to agree that there is a higher power in the universe. Studies show that this universal belief is real. Polls conducted in 2005 by *Newsweek and Beliefnet*[69], provide us with further insight.

In this poll, people were asked, "Do you believe that God created the universe?" The results show that *80 percent* of people believe this is true. Of the people questioned, 80 percent said they believe the universe was "created by God"; only 10 percent stated that it was "not created by God"; 9 percent were uncertain and stated, "I don't know"; only 1 percent said they "don't believe in God." Overwhelmingly, people do believe that God exists.

In the same way, people have a common belief that humans have a spiritual soul. When people were asked, "What happens when we die?" only 6 percent of people gave an answer that suggested there is no soul that lives beyond this physical life; 67 percent said they believe "the soul goes to heaven"; 13 percent believe there is no heaven or hell, but that the soul does live on in some kind of spiritual realm; 5 percent stated that the soul lives on through reincarnation. Remarkably, only 6 percent said that when we die, "it's all over; there is no soul."

What effect do these spiritual beliefs have on our lives? When people were asked, "Why do you practice religion?"

nearly all responses involved a connection to God or a "greater good": 30 percent said their religious beliefs helped them "be a better person and live a moral life"; 39 percent said their beliefs helped "forge a personal relationship with God"; 17 percent said it helped them "find peace and happiness"; 10 percent reported their spiritual beliefs help them "connect with something larger than self," while 8 percent said they provided "life with meaning and structure." Clearly, the pursuit of God involves our pursuit for goodness in our life.

Not only do people believe in God and the spiritual realm, but they also believe that prayer, meditation and other spiritual and religious practices play a major role in our physical health and the healing process. In 1998, the Harvard Medical School sponsored a conference called Spirituality and Healing in Medicine in which one report cited that 86 percent of Americans in general believe in the healing power of prayer, while a full 99 percent of family physicians stated they believe in prayer as a healing force.[70] Overwhelmingly, people believe God has the ability to intervene in our physical lives.

While socially there seems to be some reservation about the belief in God and a spiritual realm, the results of studies show that the opposite is true—people believe (a) that there is a spiritual realm in which God exists, (b) we are spiritual beings with a soul, (c) people seek God as a source of "goodness" in their life and (d) the spiritual realm can impact our physical world. These are important details that help us understand the significance of the *Law of Contribution*.

The *Law of Contribution* Could Be a Spiritual Law

When you consider the premise of the *Law of Contribution*—that humans must not be self-serving, but must contribute

to the needs of others in order to obtain personal fulfillment—
the idea runs true to the one common universal spiritual value
endorsed by virtually all religions: the promotion of the greater
good for all humankind. This is commonly distilled into a well-
known idea—The Golden Rule. Its original text is found in the
Bible in Matthew 7:12, which states, "Do for others what you
would like them to do for you. This is a summary of all that is
taught in the law and the prophets." This is the oldest universal
spiritual principle for guiding human behavior, and it requires
that we consider and value the needs of others.

The guiding principle to "do for others" is seen by most religions to be an all-encompassing rule for human interaction—it sum-
marizes the intent of all the other "do and don'ts." For example, in
the Rabbinical writings, written sometime between the first and sixth
century A.D., Hillel wrote, "What is hateful to you don't do to another. This is the whole Torah; the rest is commentary."

The Bible suggests the same in the book of Romans when it
states, "If you love your neighbor you will fulfill all the requirements of God's law. For the commandments against adultery and
murder and stealing and coveting—and any other commandment—are all summed up in this one commandment: 'Love your
neighbor as yourself.'"[71]

This one great spiritual virtue seems to support the primary principle behind the *Law of Contribution*; we must contribute to the needs
of others. Clearly, this spiritual truth serves to connect us with goodness
and promote the greater good for all. Many historical documents illustrate that the *Law of Contribution* is founded on ancient spiritual values that have been understood throughout the centuries. Some of the
greatest spiritual leaders have promoted the importance of this concept.

Jesus himself encouraged people to understand the idea that what you get in life is a reflection of what you give:

Do not judge others, and you will not be judged. Do not condemn others, or it will all come back against you. Forgive others, and you will be forgiven. Give, and you will receive. Your gift will return to you in full—pressed down, shaken together to make room for more, running over, and poured into your lap. The amount you give will determine the amount you get back.[72]

He also suggested that God sees all—that God himself rewards those who give. Jesus stated, "Give your gifts in secret, and your father, who knows all secrets, will reward you"[73]

King Solomon was King of Israel in about 970 B.C. He was regarded as one of the wisest and wealthiest men to ever live. Solomon wrote a book of proverbs—wise sayings to serve as practical advice. He believed giving was the key to becoming wealthy, but warned that being stingy may produce the opposite effect. He said, "It is possible to give freely and become more wealthy, but those who are stingy will lose everything."[74]

Another of King Solomon's famous proverbs illustrates the empty results of an inward-focused life: "When a bird sees a trap being set, it stays away. But not these people! They set an ambush for themselves; they booby-trap their own lives! Such is the fate of all who are greedy for gain. It ends up robbing them of life."[75]

Paul, one of the twelve disciples of Jesus, wrote the book of Philippians around A.D. 61. In it, he provided warnings to avoid self-absorption and to remember to help others: "Don't push your way to the front; don't sweet-talk your way to the top. Put yourself aside, and help others get ahead. Don't be obsessed with getting your own advantage. Forget yourselves long enough to lend a helping hand."[76]

What's the Message?

Throughout history, there seems to be a common spiritual theme: that we have an obligation to help one another. It is as if we are charged by God to serve others, to help others, to care for others, and in doing so, to promote the greater good. We are reminded to uphold the great universal spiritual truth: "Do for others." When we live with an outward focus and contribute to the needs of others, we cooperate with a code of human conduct that appears to have been set down by God. When we cooperate with the *Law of Contribution*, the benefits we receive may be derived from our collaboration with a higher power most people seem to agree exists.

The *Law of Contribution* may provide us with a practical way to cooperate with a significant spiritual value. If God is good and wants us to live a good life, then the *Law of Contribution* helps us understand how to do that. The greatest of benefits may be the awakening of our spiritual self, resulting in a greater sense of peace, happiness and meaning in life.

The significance this principle has in our lives is illustrated in the parable of the Rich Man and Lazarus.

Spiritual Life and Death

There was once a rich man who wore expensive clothes, ate the best food and lived in luxury every day. But a poor beggar named Lazarus was brought to the gate of the rich man's house, where he waited, hoping to get a meal from the scraps that fell from the rich man's table. His body was covered with sores, and dogs kept coming up to lick them.

Eventually the poor man died, and angels took him to heaven where he sat next to Abraham. The rich man also died and was buried. But the rich man was sent to hell, where he suffered terribly. From hell, he looked up and far off, saw Abraham with Lazarus at his side. He called out to Abraham, "Have pity on me! Send Lazarus to dip his finger in water and touch my tongue. I'm suffering terribly in this fire." Abraham answered, "My friend, remember that while you lived, you had everything good, and Lazarus had everything bad. Now he is happy, and you are in pain. And besides, there is a deep chasm between us, and no one from either side can cross over."

This brief parable illustrates the spiritual death we experience when we refuse to see and serve the needs of those who are right in front of us. The story illustrates that the rich man was separated from heaven, not because he was rich, but because he refused to see and serve the obvious needs of the man on his doorstep. Every day, the rich man had the opportunity to contribute, but refused to do so. He was so consumed with his own satisfaction that he was unable to see the obvious need right in front of him.

When we refuse to recognize our responsibility to help those in need, we cut ourselves off from the source of spiritual life. That is the message of this short story. The rich man was separated from heaven by a great chasm and suffered without comfort. In the same way, when we ignore the needs of those in our lives, we cut ourselves off from the spiritual connection that can bring us greater personal fulfillment. We violate the greatest of spiritual laws and suffer a kind of spiritual death when we become so self-focused that we are unable to *see* the needs of the people in our world.

Life's Great Battle

Perhaps the command to care for others is such a significant spiritual virtue because it is the basis upon which we are meant to engage in life's greatest battle—the battle between good and evil. Consider the evidence.

Although we cannot see what goes on in the spiritual realm, we can observe the results. Just like we can't see the wind, but we can see the effects of the wind, we can't see the spiritual realm, but we do see "good" and we do see "evil," and we see the effects of both forces in the world. The spiritual realm can be seen as the arena of life in which the great battle between good and evil is fought.

Much of the world loves sport and the battle of competition. Perhaps nothing unites people more than the great battles fought at the Super Bowl, the World Cup or the Stanley Cup. Weekly, thousands of people gather in stadiums to cheer for and pledge their allegiance to their local team. Millions watch TV to do the same. Around the world, nations support and stand behind their athletes. There is a near universal attraction to a fierce battle with the possibility of "victory" for the person or team that overcomes an adversary.

As much as we enjoy a good battle, we fail to see that we are competitors engaged in the greatest and oldest battle of all time.

We are engaged, each and every day, in the spiritual battle between good and evil. If you doubt this battle exists, I'd like you to consider the duality of the events of September 11, 2001.

Only pure evil could be responsible for the creation of the thought and action that resulted in men choosing to fly those planes into the World Trade Center, resulting in the destruction of thousands of lives and families. Yet on that same day, only love could be responsible for the remarkable acts of courage that drove people to run into those buildings to save whom they could. Only love could drive people to sacrifice their own lives in the pursuit of saving others. In a period of a few hours, we saw the spiritual presence of both good and evil forces in our world.

Everyday life provides us with evidence that this battle is ongoing. We can watch the evening news and observe the obvious acts of evil. Yet we can turn off our TV and enjoy the love between us and our spouse, children and family. Daily, we can see acts of hate and the opposing acts of kindness. We can see the results of evil and the results of good all around us.

Clearly, there are good and evil forces at work in our world. I believe the promotion of good is the only way to overcome the presence of evil. We do not *defeat* evil—we *displace* evil by doing good. The *Law of Contribution* is the primary force behind the promotion of good and the battle for good over evil. This law drives us to good actions and to considering and contributing to the needs of others. Inward and selfish actions drive evil thoughts and actions. It appears as though the *Law of Contribution* is a significant spiritual law that is active in the battle of good over evil.

Evil seeks to bring us down, limit us and make us fearful and depressed. It entices us to harbor bitterness, anger and resentment that destroy us emotionally and physically. It works to destroy loving relationships and families. It seeks all forms of destruction: financial, emotional, physical, mental and spiritual. It does this with the promotion of excessive inward thoughts and actions.

Conversely, the greater good is upheld by outward acts, which help us grow and flourish and become all that we can be. Outward-focused acts encourage love, significance, value and respect. They help us experience emotional and physical health and encourage thoughts and actions that make health possible. Outward acts displace evil by nurturing goodness in our life.

When we see evil and good in this light, we must choose a side. I see contribution clearly on the side of good. We must actively participate in the game of life, and if we want to win, that participation requires contribution. And so, I join in the great battle of life and choose the promotion of good over evil. Will you?

Chapter 13
Why We Don't Contribute
Lie #1: Giving Doesn't Work

Life is not fair. This I can tell you for sure. We can all think of examples of things that have happened, either to us or to others, which support the belief that "Life is not fair." However, we cannot apply this thinking to the principle of giving and contributing in life. If we do, then it prevents us from contributing and robs us of the benefits we would otherwise gain. In fact, if we don't contribute, we simply fail to live to our potential and fail to achieve anything of real value.

If we buy the lie that "Giving doesn't work," then it's because we are focused on experiences in life where we have found this to be true. I, too, can provide you with several examples from my own life where this has happened. Unfortunately, when we measure results only in the short term and stop contributing, we do not experience the benefits that come when we follow this law regardless of the short-term results.

There is, perhaps, no better story to illustrate this point than that of my good friend, Gary the Giver.

Gary is one of the most outward-focused people I know. In fact, it is his lifestyle that helped me understand the *Law of Contribution*. Without having witnessed his behavior, I would not have been able to understand this law. He modeled it for me.

Gary is about 50 years old and the owner of a small business. Externally, he seems like a pretty average guy. Nothing he has or does is extravagant—however, what he has achieved in life is re-markable, especially when you examine how he did it.

Gary and his partner, Sly Steve, owned and operated a busi-ness together for nearly 20 years. Gary established strong bonds with his employees and always supported his people. He was considerate of others and really did try to meet people's needs. As a result, his employees honored him with many years of loyal service. Several of the company's core employees worked for Gary since the inception of the business.

Approximately ten years ago, Gary and Steve sold their busi-ness to a large public company. They both agreed to remain with the organization under contract as senior managers for an initial period of two years. Under the new ownership, Steve filled the role of general manager, and Gary acted as the regional sales manager. It was during that time that I met Gary.

When I first met him, I wanted to become involved in their indus-try and he agreed to give me the opportunity. I quickly saw that peo-ple who worked for Gary enjoyed the experience. He seemed to have a genuine care for and interest in others. This outward attitude resulted in Gary having many personal contacts in the industry. No matter what the circumstance he found himself in, he was able to pick up the phone and call a friend or business associate who was able to help him. Gary had a circle of resources—people he could call on—because he went out of his way to help others. People were willing to help him because they knew they could call on *him* whenever they needed. He would usually contribute more than he took from the relationship.

As the two-year contract with the new ownership came near its end, Steve decided he would retire and an agreement was made that Gary would extend his contract and remain employed as the new general manager of the business. The hand-off was to take place in January of the following year. For several months prior, Gary was preparing in many ways for his new, extended role. However, as the time approached, he sensed that Steve and the directors of the public company began to distance themselves from him. Gary noticed they were not communicating with him as openly as before.

In January, when the expected hand-off was to take place, Gary was fired. It turned out that Sly Steve had decided he was not ready to retire, and the public company chose not to retain the expense of both managers. Sly Steve, after 20 years of working with Gary, blindsided him for the sake of an additional short-term employment contract. The employees in the company, me included, were stunned. If there was ever an example of life not being fair, this was it. This was not fair.

It would appear as though the *Law of Contribution* did not hold true in the life of Gary the Giver. He did not "get what he gave." Gary gave and gave and gave for 20 years, and after it all, he got pushed out of his own company, at a time when he was not ready to retire. It is at this point in life that it would become very easy to buy the lie, "Giving doesn't work." However, Gary's belief in a greater truth helps us understand the power of the *Law of Contribution*.

Although Gary was obviously hurt by this action, he did not stop living an outward-focused life. He remained true to his character. He kept helping people and maintained his usual interest and concern for others.

Two years later, Gary started his own business—an exact duplicate of the business from which he had been fired. In the meantime, Sly Steve had retired from his position with the public company, and since that time, the new management had done nothing but lose money. The parent company lost interest in this bleeding division and needed help. Guess whom they called? That's right—Gary!

Gary discussed the situation with them, and after several meetings, the public company agreed to simply *give* the company back to him. That's right! They essentially *gave* it back to him. They could not figure out how to make it work, so they thought it best to get rid of it rather than continue losing money. However, Gary knew exactly how to make this business work. He took the original business back and merged it with his new company, forming a business that was now larger than the original company he and Steve had owned. Only now, Gary was the sole owner. Today, that business produces approximately five times the revenue than the best year he and Steve ever achieved in their original joint partnership.

When a person remains true to the *Law of Contribution*, the Law will remain true to you. Gary did not buy the lie that "Giving does not work." Giving does work, and people like Gary know we simply need to persist and continue giving. Those who persist have stories like Gary's to tell.

When people give and don't get back, they can often be tempted to buy the lie. It is that lie that causes us to make incorrect assumptions about life itself. A lie is a *deception*. A deception leads us down a wrong path. The intention of a deception is a trick—a misleading thought that takes us where we don't want to go.

When we say, "Giving doesn't work," it's because we ask the question, "*Did I get what I deserved*?" and we answer in anger to ourselves, "*NO!*" It is at that very moment that we have gone astray. We have asked the wrong question. As a result, we have received an answer that can lead us into wrong action, unhealthy thoughts and attitudes that slowly steal our joy, peace and potential. Perhaps at that precise moment we did not get what we deserved, but by asking the wrong question, we have made a critical error. When we ask, "Did I get what I deserve?" we focus on ourselves, turn inward and begin to develop an attitude that prevents us from contributing.

Great people are not consumed with what they *get*—they are consumed with what they can *give*. Learning to stop judging whether or not you have received what you deserve will prevent you from stooping to the level of underachievers. You will notice in life that people who constantly ask, "Did I get what I deserved?" are rarely the people living in abundance. These people are often complainers, frequently angry and very rarely satisfied. They are not happy, joyful or significant people. Great people, on the other hand, are not concerned with what they get, because their life is focused on what they are giving and contributing. That is what makes them great people. That is what made Gary "successful." It's that same attitude that drives all truly successful people.

When we think of great people, we think of names like Mother Teresa, Martin Luther King, Jr., Nelson Mandela and Jesus Christ. How often do you think these people asked the question, "Am I getting what I deserve?" in the midst of their struggle? When Martin Luther King, Jr., had his house bombed, when he was put in jail, when he received death threats—all in the name of justice—did he stop and ask, "Am I getting what I deserve right now?" While Nelson Mandela sat in jail year after year because of his determination to end racism in South Africa, did he ask, "Am I getting what I deserve?" When Mother Teresa spent day after day, year after year working to help the starving and poverty-stricken people of India, did she get up in the morning and ask herself, "Am I getting what I deserve?" When Jesus Christ was arrested, brutally beaten and savagely nailed to a cross, were his words from the cross, "I did not deserve this"? Hardly. Yet somehow, the lives of these people sing with victory, achievement and significance. The outstanding characteristic of all these people is how they poured themselves out prodigiously on behalf of others, of their utter selflessness—of their being so outward.

You see, what makes people significant is their conviction to contribute, regardless of the short-term outcome. If we want to reap the benefits of the *Law of Contribution*, we need to learn to give without judging whether it is working or not. You cannot judge the reality of whether or not this law works based on individual circumstances. Such a short-term focus is not sufficient to reflect reality. Contributing for a brief time and then saying, "This doesn't work" is failing to understand the significance of the law to impact your life. When you give, you promote the greater good, you become a certain kind of person, you meet the needs of others, you become significant and, eventually, your life begins to overflow with abundance. If we say, "Giving doesn't work," we live with a very short-sighted perspective.

We live in a world that promotes instant everything. We believe we are entitled to get what we want whenever we want it.

But that's not how real life works. If you judge the results you get by the instant response, you'll form incorrect theories about how to act in life. Why are we so consumed with getting what we deserve? Why are we so offended when things are not "fair"?

We only get what we really want and need in life when we learn to contribute and give without asking, "Am I getting what I deserve?" When we stop evaluating the short-term responses and commit to a larger principle, we set in motion a law that must reward us.

The Biblical story and character of Joseph provides perhaps the best example in history of what can be gained from an unwavering commitment to this law. (Whether or not you believe this Biblical story is a report of actual historical events or simply an interesting fable does not matter for the purpose of this illustration.)

Joseph was born in the land of Canaan in about 1915 B.C., the favorite son of his father Jacob. Every day, Joseph wore his coat of many colors, a special gift from his father that was a constant reminder of his father's special love for him. His eleven brothers, who all worked with Joseph in the fields, hated him because they knew he was their father's favorite.

When Joseph was about 17 years old, he began having dreams in which he held a position of power. He told his brothers about his dreams: "We were out in the field tying up bundles of grain. My bundle stood up and then your bundles all gathered around and bowed before it!" Naturally, this fuelled the brothers' anger toward him.

In fact, the brothers became so angry with Joseph that they conspired to kill him. One day when they were all in the fields together, far from their father's home, they decided that instead of killing him, they would sell him as a slave to an oncoming band of traders passing through on its way to Egypt. Joseph found himself going from a position of father's favorite to slave on his way to Egypt. He had every reason to ask himself, "Am I getting what I deserve?"

Once in Egypt, the traders sold Joseph to a man named Potiphar, an officer of Pharaoh, king of Egypt. Now, you can imagine that Joseph had no good reason to want to contribute in his situation. However, the story reports that "Joseph had success in everything he did." Potiphar was so impressed with what Joseph had been doing that he put him in charge of his entire household and entrusted him with all of his business dealings. After some time, Joseph had complete administrative responsibility over everything Potiphar owned. Now, this type of accomplishment does not come from a person sitting around saying, "This is not fair; I do not deserve to be a slave." He took care of the needs of his owner and was rewarded.

But Joseph's story is one in which just when he thinks things are getting better, they get worse again. It turns out that Joseph was a good-looking guy and Potiphar's wife happened to notice—so much so that she asked him to sleep with her. However, because of Joseph's great respect for his owner, he refused. In anger, Potiphar's wife set up Joseph and publicly accused him of trying to rape her.

After hearing his wife's version of the story, Potiphar was furious and threw Joseph into prison. Once again, Joseph found himself the victim of unfair treatment. He certainly had every good reason to say, "I'm not getting what I deserve." Joseph sat in jail for *years*. Imagine that—falsely accused, wasting away in jail. But based on how Joseph responded, we get the strong feeling that he was not spending his time ruminating about how unfair this was. It's reported that the chief jailer put Joseph in charge of all the other prisoners and over everything that happened in the prison. It didn't seem to matter what the situation was, Joseph found ways to contribute.

Some time later, the Pharaoh's chief cup-bearer and chief baker ended up in jail with Joseph. Each of these men had dreams that troubled them. Joseph was able to correctly interpret their dreams and provide them with their meaning. When Joseph told the cup-bearer his dream was a sign that the cup-bearer would soon be back serving the king, he was elated. The cup-bearer promised Joseph that once he was set free, he would ask Pharaoh to set Joseph free. Although the cup-bearer agreed to plead Joseph's case to Pharaoh, once released, he promptly forgot his promise. Joseph's hope that his helping the cup-bearer would gain him a chance for freedom was quickly destroyed.

Two years later, King Pharaoh had troubling dreams. He called on his magicians and wise men, but no one could interpret the meaning of the dreams. Just then, the cup-bearer remembered, and told Pharaoh, that Joseph had been able to correctly interpret his dream. Pharaoh immediately called for Joseph and told him his dreams. Joseph correctly interpreted the dreams, which were a warning of difficult economic times to come. The dreams meant that the next seven years would be a period of great prosperity throughout Egypt. However, the following seven years would consist of great famine that would destroy the land.

Joseph told Pharaoh, "My suggestion is that you find the wisest man in Egypt and put him in charge of a nationwide program." He suggested that they collect one-fifth of all the crops during the seven good years and gather them into storehouses, so there would be food saved for the time of famine.

Joseph's suggestions were well received by Pharaoh and his advisors. As they discussed who should be appointed for the job, Pharaoh said, "Who could do it better than Joseph?" Pharaoh said, "You are the wisest man in the land. I hereby appoint you to direct this project. You will manage my household and organize all my people. Only I will have a rank higher than yours. I hereby put you in charge of the entire land of Egypt."

Essentially, Joseph became the second in command over all of Egypt. Years later, when the famine had spread, Joseph had large stores of grain. Jacob, Joseph's father, heard that there was food in Egypt, so he sent his sons, Joseph's brothers, to Egypt to buy grain. There, his brothers bowed before Joseph to buy grain, just like Joseph's dream had predicted some 15 years earlier.

Even though Joseph faced many years of disappointments and situations in which he had every right to ask, "Am I getting what I deserve?" he continued to contribute, and as a result, he rose to the top in every environment he found himself. Joseph was sold into slavery—betrayed by his brothers. He was falsely accused—betrayed by his master's wife. He was forgotten—betrayed, for two years by the cup-bearer. All the same, he somehow refused to focus on how *unfair* his situation was; instead, he *served* his way to the top in each of those situations. Perhaps it was that attitude that helped Joseph become the man he was when he finally stood in front of the King of Egypt. Perhaps it was that character that shone so brightly in Joseph that caused Pharaoh to say, "You are the wisest man in Egypt."

Did Joseph get what he deserved? In the end, he got more than he could have possibly imagined. He received what he did precisely because he refused to buy the lie, "Giving doesn't work." Like all great people, he refused to focus on the wrong question, "Am I getting what I deserve?" Instead, he lived by a law that must and did reward him.

The next time you hear people complaining about something, listen to the real issue. The underlying theme will nearly always be, "This isn't fair" and "I am not getting what I deserve." This attitude promotes the lie that "Giving doesn't work." "He got a raise and I did not"; "I gave my company years of service and just got laid-off"; "My boss treated me unfairly, despite all I do for him"; "I always help my friend, but she's never there for me when I need her." "Not fair, not fair, not fair!" When this happens, we get caught asking the wrong question, "Did I get what I deserve?" Don't get caught in the cycle. Commit to live a life of contribution, regardless of the short-term outcome.

I have a good personal friend—Intelligent Ian—who told me about his experience with this principle. Ian has always been committed to serving and contributing to the needs of his employer. In one particular position, he recalls that his contribution was a direct cause of great profit for the company and his boss. Yet many times, he reported feeling that his work was not appreciated. Despite his great successes, his boss would often get in one of those moods where he became aggressive and angry. It was not because of anything Ian did; however, because Ian worked closely with him, he would often get caught in the crossfire. Ian admits that early in his career, it was easy for him to ask, "Did I deserve this"? Each time he asked, he immediately found the answer to be "No."

In such a situation, it would have been easy for Ian to allow himself to become angry and stop contributing, believing that "Giving doesn't work." The other option was to recognize that he was committed to a higher principle, and that he would not let brief moments of less than ideal behavior from others change his outlook. He chose to recognize that perhaps his boss was under a great deal of stress and simply needed help. Instead of becoming bitter, he attempted to help his boss all the more and sought to contribute to his needs. Ian found that not only did he feel better, but that his boss eventually began to approach him differently. I can only guess that it becomes difficult to be aggressive with someone who is simply and honestly trying to help you.

Do-It Don had a similar experience whereby the short-term results of his contributions did not reflect the long-term benefit he eventually received. Don was one of the businessmen I taught this principle to, and he was excited about finding opportunities to contribute. He knew he had the resources to make a difference in the lives of others. His first opportunity to contribute came when a girl at his son's school was involved in a tragic accident that left her paralyzed. He looked into the situation to find out that the family was in great financial need, and the medical expenses resulting from the accident were making an already horrific situation even more of a nightmare for the parents. As a result, he decided to make a significant cash donation to the family to help them in their time of need.

Not long after, a friend of his was working on a business concept, but lost all of the data because he was working with a very old laptop computer. When Don found out what had happened, he purchased a new laptop for his friend. His friend was touched, and the new computer made it possible for him to continue working on his project while he traveled. Don felt good about the positive impact he was making on others.

Next, Don was asked by his boss to prepare a business plan for a venture the company was considering. With his new outlook to contribute as much as possible, Don decided to "go the extra mile" and spent a considerable amount of his own time performing research and preparing the presentation. The result was fantastic. The board decided to proceed, based on his recommendations, and the results proved to be exactly as he had anticipated.

Just as Don was feeling like this new lifestyle of contributing was working, things began to change. He received notice from the government that his taxes had been miscalculated and that a significant amount of back taxes was due. His friend, for whom he had purchased the laptop, was incredibly disinterested when Don attempted to discuss his tax problem with him. Then it was his company's year-end and time for annual bonuses. Don was expecting a significant bonus because he had produced terrific results for the company that year, and his "going the extra mile" for the company had worked out well for his boss. He was shocked when he received his bonus—a small fraction of what was promised to him.

Don's reaction was, "This contribution stuff doesn't work! I gave money to the needy family, I purchased a laptop for my friend, I helped my boss and look at how I'm being rewarded." In his discussion with me, I reminded him that the short-term circumstances were not a reflection of how he would benefit if he continued to contribute. So he did. The result? The work he had done for his boss turned out to have a significant impact in his industry and was recognized by another company. That company offered him an employment contract that provided Don with significant financial benefit. The financial reward far exceeded the combined total of his tax bill, his donation to the needy family and the cost of the laptop. While this didn't happen overnight, he did recognize the benefits of continuing to contribute to the needs of those around him. He finally admitted to me that once he stopped evaluating whether or not the giving was "working," he began to enjoy helping others. He didn't object to the end result and benefits he eventually received either.

It's easy for us to buy the lie that giving doesn't work. However, it is these kinds of everyday situations that serve to shape our character and regulate the results we get in life. A daily commitment to contribution and a belief that giving really does work will produce similar results in your life. It really is true, *"You get what you want when you give to meet others' needs."*

Does It Work?

People who follow the *Law of Contribution* find that it works. From my experience in discovering and slowly learning how to apply the law in my life, I can tell you it has changed me and produced wonderful results in my life. However, it does require a commitment to live this way. It is not a tactic that can be applied for a brief period of time.

I can also tell you that there were many times in the past few years where I came close to burning this manuscript and proclaiming, "This doesn't work." Often, I found that when I tried to be outward, in the short term I did not get results I believed were "fair." What I learned was that we cannot say this does not work based on one incident in which we "gave" and did not "get" fair treatment in return. A lifestyle of contributing, a consistent outward attitude, will produce a bountiful harvest in our life. We do reap what we sow.

Chapter 14
Why We Don't Contribute
Lie #2: I Don't Matter

One of the primary reasons people fail to contribute is due to the belief that their individual attitudes and actions don't make much of a difference in their world. If you believe this may be true, then you buy the lie that "I don't matter." When this happens, you fail to contribute to your potential, and as a result, fall short of experiencing a full and abundant life. Perhaps most important of all, if you believe what you do doesn't matter, you fail to realize the true potential you have to offer others. You fail to understand the truth—that outward-focused actions can make a significant impact on your world.

You will recall from the first chapter that our decisions and behaviors are greatly influenced by others. People naturally do what they see others doing, especially when they believe they might benefit from taking a similar action. That also means other people might do what they see *you* doing. Yes, you! Let me explain.

Some time ago, I made a change in my diet, stopped drinking coffee and started eating much healthier foods. People who know me noticed and asked me why. I explained that I had been feeling quite tired, had done some research, and discovered that there were some things about the way I was eating that were affecting how I was feeling. I also explained that since I had made the change, I had lost weight and had begun feeling much better. Immediately, several people wanted to know what I had done and were extremely interested in starting a similar program.

Many of them admitted that they too were feeling poorly and looking for a solution. A few people even contacted the same trainer I was using, hoping to get similar results. By just my mentioning what I had done, several other people took note and chose to follow my actions, although I had no intention for this to happen. This is a simple example of how one person can affect the actions of others.

Every day, people take cues from each other in ways similar to this example. Often, one person's actions can affect many others. A few years ago, I started doing some consulting work for a rather small company. When I first met the employees, there were only a few administrative women working in the office. However, as the company grew, it hired more administrative staff and more women joined the office. When there were only a few women, they dressed rather modestly. Then, at one point, a particular woman was hired who dressed in a trendier fashion. The other women obviously took notice and started following suit, dressing in a similar way. Within a short period of time, virtually all of the women dressed up to the standard set by the one woman. The women even started shopping for clothes together during their lunch hour. In this case, one person unintentionally affected how a small group of people decided to dress.

In the same way, your attitudes and actions make an impact on those around you. When you are outward, your actions breed outward behavior in others. When you are inward, your actions breed inward behaviors in others. Your actions can trigger good and healthy results for others, or they can trigger destructive outcomes. Let's consider the example of a day in the life of Ed the Executive.

Ed is a business executive. He represents the typical North American profile: married, with two kids and a dog. Monday mornings are always a bit of a rush for Ed, and this particular Monday morning is an especially bad one. His wife, Sherry, forgot to set the alarm clock (at least that's his perspective), and he knows his schedule at work that day will be hectic and stressful. Being late won't make his day any easier. He is insensitive toward his wife and both kids as he races out the door—mentally preoccupied with the coming day's events.

Sherry doesn't feel she did anything to deserve such treatment and becomes upset by her husband's rude behavior. The children notice her unhappiness as they get ready for school, making their day a little less pleasant than normal.

Ed heads off into traffic, and because he is later than normal, finds that the roads are significantly busier than when he normally drives to work. He becomes stressed, even a bit angry, thinking about how his day will be affected because his wife forgot to set the alarm clock. As a result, he drives with less patience and caution than normal, cutting off another driver in his attempt to get to work on time.

The other driver takes exception to Ed's driving and becomes extremely upset, waving his fist and following Ed closely to ensure Ed notices. By the time the other driver gets to work, he is visibly upset by the encounter and proceeds to tell everyone around the coffee machine about the "idiot" who cut him off in traffic. Others in his office are affected by his negative emotions. Just as he settles into his workday, a customer happens to call him with a problem for which his level of patience has been seriously limited by the morning's events. "Can this day get any worse?" he thinks.

During the day, Sherry has coffee with her friend Angela and complains about how thoughtless Ed can be. This reminds Angela about something her husband did a few days ago that upset her in a similar way, and soon the two women are engaged in a full-out story-swapping session about their miserable husbands. Both of them return home from coffee feeling even less satisfied with their partners than before. When Angela's husband gets home, he's treated with a cold shoulder without realizing why.

Meanwhile, by the time Ed gets to work, he is racing with negative emotions. His employees and coworkers recognize that this is going to be another one of those bad days for Ed, and an even worse day for those who are forced to share the workplace with him.

In this example, the way Ed chose to approach the day had a profound effect on those in his world. His wife, his kids, the stranger on the road, his employees, his coworkers, his wife's friend, and even his wife's friend's husband were all impacted by Ed's actions. The ripple effect of inward behaviors spread like a bad virus. One person's actions can cause a chain reaction, disturbing many other people. However, in the same way that Ed produced a destructive result, you can produce a significant benefit in the lives of others in your world by being outward focused.

When you take the time to consider and contribute to the needs of others in your world, the simplest of actions can make a huge impact. You never know how your contribution might make a difference in the lives of others. In one case, a manager literally saved the life of an employee with a simple outward-focused gesture.

A leadership coach and former Chief Solutions Officer at Yahoo, Tim Sanders urges managers and supervisors to let their subordinates know how much they appreciate them. Sanders advocates leading through loving in his book *Love Is the Killer App*. He often tells the story of a young manager named Steve, who was challenged by Sanders' message.

Steve resolved to visit each of his employees, all six of whom he had not seen face to face in over six months, even though they worked in the same building and on the same floor. Steve wanted to tell each of them how much he appreciated them and name one thing they did with excellence.

After the visit from Steve, one of his software engineers, Lenny, presented him with an Xbox gaming console. Steve was taken aback, as he knew Lenny had taken pay cuts over the last year. But he was more surprised to learn that the money had come from the sale of a nine-millimeter pistol—a pistol Lenny had bought months earlier with the intention of killing himself. Lenny told him of his mother's death the previous year and of his ensuing loneliness and depression:

> *I started a routine every night after work: eating a bowl of ramen, listening to Nirvana, and getting the gun out. It took almost a month to get the courage to put the bullets in the gun. It took another couple of months to get used to the feeling of the barrel of the gun on the top of my teeth. For the last few weeks, I was putting ever so slight pressure on the trigger, and I was getting so close, Steve—so close.*
>
> *Last week, you freaked me out. You came into my cubicle, put your arm around me, and told me you appreciated me because I turn in all my projects early, and that helps you sleep at night. You also said that I have a great*

sense of humor over e-mail and that you are glad I came into your life.

That night I went home, ate ramen, and listened to Nirvana—and when I got the gun out, it scared me silly for the first time. All I could think about was what you said—that you were glad I came into your life.

The next day I went back to the pawnshop and sold the gun. I remembered that you had said you wanted the Xbox more than anything, but with a new baby at home could not afford it. So, for my life, you get this game. Thanks, boss.[77]

Clearly, one person can have a significant effect on the lives of others. I would call saving a life significant! The smallest of contributions, even a few sincere words, has the power to inject life into the lives of others. The return on investment when you give to others is immeasurable. The benefits cannot be weighed! Your contribution matters!

We each have a unique position in life. We each have access to a very select group of people that we can impact with our contribution. Those people *need* contributions from others. They need contributions from *you.*

You have the ability to be one of the most influential forces in the lives of the people around you. The importance of one person's effect on the path of another person's life cannot be overstated. In the course of our lives, there is a small handful of people that has had the ability to really impact our destiny. Someone who cared—a close friend, a coach, a teacher, a boss, a parent—likely changed the direction of your life. Many highly successful people can make the connection between what they have become and the actions or attitudes of one particular person who altered their life.

Consider James Cameron, master filmmaker and director of the films *The Terminator, Aliens, True Lies* and *Titanic*. What one person ignited the self-confidence that enabled him to overcome and achieve in life? His grade 11 biology teacher, Mr. McKenzie. Cameron says,

> *Teachers can be absolutely critical at the right moment in your life…. The critical moment for me was in the 11th grade.*
>
> *Sometimes it's only just one comment that they can make. I was talking to this man, my biology teacher, and he said, "I've seen your aptitude tests…and we believe that you have unlimited potential." Now I don't know if he'd ever seen the tests and I don't know if any of the data indicated that, but hearing that, and knowing that somebody somewhere believed that I could go accomplish something, was a big contributor to the self-confidence necessary to overcome all of these things later…. Sometimes it only takes one person to tell you that you can do something and you take it to heart. Otherwise I wouldn't have remembered it all these years, and I remember where the conversation took place.*[78]

Where did Frederick W. Smith, founder of Federal Express, learn about the persistence it would take to become a successful entrepreneur? From one person—his high school football coach. Smith recalls,

> *My high school football coach was very important to me, in setting me straight on a few things. He was a little guy who was a great football player at Georgia Tech, and he just was indefatigable. He just would never, ever say die. He absolutely proved to me that persistence was a very big part of making it in life. I never forgot that lesson.*[79]

How did best-selling author John Grisham first conceive his desire to write? From one person—his high school English teacher—Francis McGuffey. When asked, "Was there a person who inspired you?" Grisham spoke of one teacher who ignited his interest in literature. He described her influence:

> *She forced us to read good books…. We weren't too thrilled to do it initially, but she taught us how to do it. Through that, I discovered some of my favorite authors, particularly John Steinbeck. I remember reading a lot of Steinbeck in high school and thinking, "I'd love to be able to write this clearly." She's still teaching, and we still correspond. She comes to my book signings in Memphis when I'm there. I send her an autographed copy of every book. We're still friends, still buddies.*[80]

Clearly, when people recognize that what they do matters, they begin to purposefully contribute to and affect the lives of others. You need not be a schoolteacher, business leader or football coach to have the opportunity to make a significant impact on your world. Even the poorest children can alter the course of history when their intentions are to help others.

Consider the life of a little girl we'll call Izzy. Sometime near the turn of the twentieth century, little Izzy wanted to go to Sunday school, but was turned away because she was told it was "full." The pastor of the church noticed her standing outside crying because she could not go in. "I can't go to Sunday school," she sobbed to the pastor.

Seeing her shabby, unkempt appearance, the pastor guessed the reason and, taking her by the hand, took her inside and found a place for her in the Sunday school class. The child was so happy they found room for her that she went to bed that night thinking of the children who have no place to go to church.

Some two years later, this child lay dead in one of the poor tenement buildings and the parents called for the kind-hearted pastor, who had befriended their daughter, to handle the final arrangements.

As her poor little body was moved, a worn and crumpled purse was found that seemed to have been rummaged from some trash dump. Inside they found 57 cents and a note scribbled in childish handwriting that read, "This is to help build the little church bigger so more children can go to Sunday school." For two years, she had saved for this offering of love. Although she had the least to offer, she wanted to give to help others.

When the pastor tearfully read that note, he was moved to take action. Carrying this note and the cracked, red pocketbook to the pulpit, he told the story of her unselfish love and devotion. He challenged his deacons to get busy and raise enough money for the larger building. By chance, a newspaper learned of the story and published it. A realtor read the story and offered the church a parcel of land worth many thousands of dollars. When told the church could not pay so much, he offered it for 57 cents.

Church members made large donations. Checks came from far and wide. Within five years, the little girl's gift, driven by her desire to help other kids go to Sunday school, had increased to $250,000, a huge sum for that time. That one action, by one little girl, had paid a large dividend. Her action influenced the pastor's action, which influenced the congregation's actions, which influenced the realtor's actions, which influenced people from all over the country. What can one little girl affect with 57 cents?

When you are in the city of Philadelphia, look up Temple Baptist Church, with a seating capacity of 3,300 and Temple

University, where hundreds of students are trained. Have a look, too, at the Good Samaritan Hospital and at a Sunday school building that houses hundreds of Sunday schoolers, so that no child in the area will ever need to be left outside during Sunday school time.

In one of the rooms of this building, you may see a picture of the sweet face of the little girl whose 57 cents made such an impact on history. Alongside of it is a portrait of her kind pastor, Dr. Russell H. Conwell, author of the book *Acres of Diamonds*.

If that little girl had bought the lie, "I don't matter," the lives of thousands of people would not have benefited in the way they have today. With 57 cents and a pure desire to help others, her attitude became contagious in a way that inspired others.

What else can one person affect? What other life-changing decisions can a single person influence? Mike Krzyzewski, "Coach K," is well known as the coach of the Duke University basketball team. At one point in his career, the Los Angeles Lakers offered him the position of head coach. This would be the ultimate objective, the pinnacle of achievement, for a person in his position. Not to mention the financial benefits—a $40 million contract offer.

Coach K called a press conference to announce his decision. The answer? No! He would remain as coach of Duke University. Why? Because of an e-mail sent to him from *one* person—whom he didn't even know. Coach said his decision was influenced by Duke student Andrew Humphries, a 19-year-old biology major. In his e-mail, Humphries recounted childhood memories of playing basketball in his driveway and pretending to hit the shot that won the national championship for Coach K.

He spoke of the pride he felt in being part of the "sixth man" student body at Duke that fills Cameron Indoor Stadium to root for their team. He closed his message with the impassioned plea, "Please still be my coach."

Krzyzewski said that Humphries' e-mail had moved him to tears and reminded him of the special bond he felt with the Duke students and his players. The coach chose to turn down a $40 million contract offer and stay at Duke, influenced by the comments from a single student.[81]

One person changed Coach K's career path and also provided opportunity for other young men at Duke University to be coached by one of basketball's greatest coaches. One person makes a difference. A poor child can make a difference. A university student can make a difference. You can make a difference.

It is regular people like you and me who make the difference. It's when people like us recognize that their contributions make an impact on the lives of others that we see all kinds of opportunities to contribute. When we go to work every day with the understanding that each day offers countless opportunities to contribute—that's when we begin to make an impact. It's those daily contributions that matter most.

Every day, contributions change our world. It's people who contribute in the simplest, most meaningful ways that make the biggest impact on the lives of others, and who ultimately benefit the most themselves. When you buy the lie, "I don't matter," you miss out on the opportunity to contribute. Not only do you not receive all the joy and satisfaction of contributing, but also the lives of many other people do not receive the benefit of what you have to offer. Don't buy the lie! You have something to offer. What you do matters, and matters a lot.

If you begin to look for opportunities to contribute every day, your life will begin to take on new meaning. When you take the time to help those around you, your outward actions can help others develop interests, skills and abilities that can alter their life. If you take action and contribute to other people at every opportunity, you will see the potential your life contains. I can tell you from personal experience that once you begin to contribute, and begin helping people, you'll see that it doesn't require all that much effort, yet each day becomes almost magical as you observe how you impact others.

There are little, yet very significant, opportunities to help people every day. Becoming the kind of person who looks for, and acts on, those opportunities will bring about a wonderful feeling to each day you approach this way. You'll never understand until you try it.

In the final chapter of this book, you will go through a short workshop to help you better understand specifically how you can live a life of contribution. For now, let me leave you with this:

> *When I was a young man, I wanted to change the world. I found it was difficult to change the world, so I tried to change my nation. When I found I could not change the nation, I began to focus on my town. I couldn't change the town and as an older man, I tried to change my family. Now, as an old man, I realize the only thing I can change is myself, and suddenly I realized that if long ago I had changed myself, I could have made an impact on my family. My family could have made an impact on our town. Their impact could have changed the nation and I could indeed have changed the world.*
>
> - Unknown

It all starts with *you*!

Chapter 15
Putting the *Law of Contribution* into Practice

Five Key Questions, Two Essential Attitudes and One FAQ

By now you can see clearly that a life of contribution produces benefits beyond measure. This chapter helps you devise your own personal action plan for living a life of contribution. It helps you focus your thoughts on the most important things you need to consider if you really want the *Law of Contribution* to work for you.

This action plan involves contemplating and answering five key questions. By answering these questions, you will discover how to become more outward focused in your everyday life.

These five questions answer one big question: "What can I do to enable my greatest possible contribution in life?" The answer to that question will enable your greatest possible life—full of love, significance and fulfillment.

Five Key Questions

1. Who Is Contributing to Me?

Even before you contemplate what you have to give and to whom, you need to identify *who* is contributing to you in your life right now. You need to answer the question, "Am I giving where I'm getting?" The surest way to ensure that others will not give to you is to take when others give, but not give back in return. Would you want to continue to give to someone who does not recognize or appreciate what you have done? Not likely. And others won't either.

Many people in your life contribute in some way to your needs and, if you fail to recognize them and give in return, you will not build bonds that ensure you continue to get your needs met. Rule #1: *Never take without giving back*. Giving back to others who give to you helps build and solidify relationships. You can't expect to get what you want from others for very long without giving back in return.

Make a list below of the people who contribute to your life. Some common and overlooked contributors are your employer, your employees, your business associates, your spouse, your parents, and your children.

_____

_____

_____

_____

Next, make a point to tell these people you appreciate what they provide you with. This must be done with sincere *words*. Not flowers with a note, not a gift, not chocolate—words. This, in itself, will make an enormous impact on the lives of these people. I did this with one of my large clients. After a brief meeting I had with the president of the company, I expressed my gratitude for his contribution in my life. He was clearly shocked and, I think, satisfied to know I was grateful for what he had done for me.

You need to recognize the people who meet your needs or who otherwise contribute to you in a meaningful way. Tell your coach how much he has helped you; tell your boss you're grateful for the opportunity she has provided you; tell your spouse how thankful you are to have him or her in your life; tell your friends how much their friendship means to you; tell your kids how proud you are of them; recognize your employees for how they contribute to your success.

One of the best places to start is with your parents. Few children recognize their parents for what they have done for them. Many parents sacrificed in ways we did not understand as children, but do understand as we get older. But when we get older, we fail to offer our parents the satisfaction of recognizing them for what they have done for us. Yet a few words could repay many sacrifices our parents so willingly made. If you are a parent, you know how much this would mean.

After expressing your gratitude with words, make a point of giving in return whenever the opportunity presents itself. When you have recognized someone with words, and then follow-up with outward actions, that person will notice. Because these simple outward-focused actions are so rare, this is the first step in making a huge impact on your world.

2. What Are My Most Powerful Resources?

You have within you something to give. You have resources that are valuable to others. Those resources must be ignited and used to be useful. You have three kinds of resources that can be used to enable your contribution in life: possessions, experience and proficiency.

First, acknowledge your most powerful *possessions*—the power to love, value, respect, honor, encourage, mentor, give, sacrifice, care, help, nurture and instruct (to only scratch the surface). The most powerful forms of giving are non-material, easy to give and cost you nothing. You have these resources and can give them anytime you choose!

Second, recognize your unique life *experience*. Everything that has happened to you in life (even the horrible things) are unique to you and make you who you are. Who you are—with your specific experiences, hurts and victories—can be used to serve or help other people. Any trial or experience you have had can become a resource that enables you to help another person in a similar situation. All of your life experiences can be redeemed for a purpose—to serve the needs of others. What resources do you have, as a result of life experiences, that you can use to help others?

Third, recognize your innate *proficiency*—your skills, abilities and strengths. You need to recognize that you have skills, abilities and talents that are uniquely yours. You are made with a certain capability, the ability to do certain things well. We each have an inventory of skills and abilities that can enable our contribution to others. By recognizing and identifying your strengths, you are better able to understand how you can contribute in life.

Your skills and abilities enable your contribution to others' needs. Your specific talents are meant to serve a specific need. The value of your special talents can only be recognized when you contribute while using them. You are designed with the ability to make a difference. When you begin purposefully using your God-given abilities to serve others, you will have taken a major step toward fulfillment.

If you don't feel like you have specific skills or abilities, or if you don't know what they are, it's not because you don't possess them; it's because you have not discovered them yet. You need to start contributing in different ways and start paying attention to what you enjoy most. This will provide you with clues to your individual strengths.

Answering the following questions will help you identify your specific skills.

What are you good at?

_____

_____

What do you enjoy?

_____

_____

What do you desire, hope for, have interest in, or dream about doing?

_____

_____

The answers to these questions will provide a good starting point for identifying your special talents and how they can be used to serve.

If you have a hard time thinking of answers, consider what you have done in the past that you felt successful at, or what particular tasks you enjoyed the most. If you can't think of answers, you need to try different things in order to uncover your strengths. They can only be discovered when you use them. The more opportunities you are willing to explore, the better chance you have of discovering your strengths.

The real tragedy of life is not in being limited to one talent, but in the failure to use that one talent.

- Edgar W. Work

Pay close attention to how it feels to do different things, and be objective about evaluating your performance. If you're not good at something, and don't enjoy it, don't sulk; just leave it alone and go on to something else.

Anything you can do well, that you enjoy doing, and that there is a demand for is worth taking seriously as a skill to develop.

Once you have identified a skill, ability or task you enjoy, you need to develop your skills. Invest in the development of your resources. Get additional education. Practice using your skills at every opportunity. Work is often the best arena in which to practice your skills and abilities.

Once you have recognized your capabilities, answer the following question:

How can you use your skills and abilities to enable your greatest contribution?

_____

_____

_____

If you don't know how to answer this question, I suggest the following:

- Contribute in every way you can, with every opportunity that presents itself.

- Keep doing the things you enjoy.

- Stop doing the things you don't enjoy.

Everyone has been made for some particular work, and the desire for that work has been put in every heart.

- Rumi

3. Where in "My World" Is My Contribution Needed?

This book culminates with the question, "Whose needs can I meet?"

You need to "see" opportunities for contribution. When you start looking, you will "see" needs. We each have a unique positioning in life and the opportunity to impact a unique group of people. The specific circle of people in "your world" is unique to you.

Who are those people placed in your life who you can contribute to?

Imagine the impact your life can make on others as you contemplate where you can contribute.

Contribution at Home

At home, your spouse and children need what you have to give. When you leave work, begin thinking about the needs of those at home. Leave work at work, and focus your mind and actions on the needs of the people in other areas of your life.

If you are keen about meeting the needs of your spouse, I would like you to do the following: Ask your partner to list all of the things he or she would like most. A bubble bath, a certain dinner or dessert, a night at the opera, hugs or kisses, time together and so on. Encourage your spouse to write these ideas out for you. Explain that you want the list so that you can try to meet these needs. I assure you that your spouse will be impressed by just your asking. Even the possibility of getting these needs met will be encouraging.

We all want our needs met. Why not meet your partner's needs and watch how excited he or she gets by your asking, and then watch what happens when you actually do it. But do not over-promise. Explain that the reality of life is that we are all busy and that you may not be able to do these things all of the time, but that you will make it a priority.

What usually happens next is that your spouse will be so impressed that he or she will ask you to write out your list of needs and wants. And this is where the true test of outward focus comes into play. You will not provide the list right away. Why? Because your object is simply to give. By not immediately providing your list, you show your actions are truly outward and your intentions are focused on the other person. Do this, and enjoy the results. You will feel good and you will notice that your partner will suddenly, and very naturally, want to please you in return.

Contribution at Work

How can you contribute at work?

_____

_____

_____

Work is the primary arena in which to develop yourself by contributing. Work takes up one-third of your life. Use it as an opportunity to improve the quality of your life. Using your talents and abilities can be innately enjoyable, and change how you view the purpose of work.

If you find that your work does not allow you to use your skills and abilities, you are probably not enjoying yourself and you need to find a way to make a change. But work can be more than a place to contribute with your skills and abilities; you can contribute to the needs of others using your possessions—the power to _love, value, respect, honor, encourage, mentor, give, sacrifice, care, help, nurture, instruct_ and so on. You may want to go back now and answer the question again, "How can you contribute at work?

Contribution in Your Community

How can you contribute to the needs of your friends and community?

_____

_____

_____

Once you look for opportunities, you will notice all kinds of needs that require your contribution. I found that once I took this mindset, I noticed needs everywhere. A flyer came to my home near Christmastime that asked for help serving the needs of the homeless. So I called to help.

When I went to church, the bulletin contained a request for help—a single mom with four children needed help with necessary renovations in her home. I have those "skills," so naturally I offered to help.

When my children complain about something, I listen carefully to what the unmet need is, and make sure I offer them what they really need most.

When you take a sincere outward focus, life will present all kinds of rewarding opportunities to make a difference in the life of others.

Imagine how your life might be if you started looking for and contributing to those in "your world."

It may seem to you conceited to suppose that you can do anything important toward improving the lot of mankind. But this is fallacy. You must believe that you can help bring about a better world. A good society is produced only by good individuals, just as truly as a majority in a presidential election is produced by the votes of single electors. Everybody can do something toward creating his own environment, kindly feelings rather than anger, reasonableness rather than hysteria, happiness rather than misery.

- Bertrand Russell

Where else in "your world" is your contribution needed?
Begin looking for opportunities where you can contribute to or
help others.

_____

_____

4. What Do I Want?

You will notice that this is the only place in this book where
I have suggested focusing on what *you* want. But now that you
have finished this book, and have a different perspective on life,
I want you to answer this question:

Make a list of what you want.

_____

_____

_____

_____

_____

In order for you to *get* what you want, you must identify
what you must *give*. Things will only come to those who contribute. Perhaps a better way to say this is, "What kind of person do you need to become, in order to get what you want?" If
you want a loving marriage, what kind of person must you become? If you want a raise, or better pay, what kind of employee
must you become? If you want to start your own business, what
talents do you need to develop? What needs will you fill? If you
want your kids to grow up to be successful, what kind of parent
must you become? Answer the question below:

What kind of person do I need to become in order to get what I want?

_____

_____

_____

_____

5. What Is My Worthy Cause?

A meaningful and purposeful life is one that joins with something greater than ourselves. If you want your life to have meaning and purpose, you need to attach it to a worthy cause. We all have some kind of cause. Our cause is what we are committed to. Some people are committed solely to their own satisfaction. They work to make money, and come home to watch TV, play golf or drink beer. Others are committed to their bodies, spending every free moment in the gym. Some people are committed to making a lot of money. Everything they do is focused on obtaining wealth.

Your cause is the primary driving force behind your actions. Having a worthy cause is to be driven by something that serves a greater good. To have a worthy cause is to be driven by something that contributes beyond self.

What are you committed to? You are going to live your life for something: what will it be? Will you make an impact and a difference?

Most worthy causes are centered on serving a greater good, the expansion of happiness, the promotion of a passion, serving others or God, a conviction, a calling or a sense of obligation.

In what areas of life are you most interested in making a difference? What convictions and values drive your actions? Is there something you have always wanted to do?

Is there something you feel obligated to accomplish or contribute toward?

Write down those ideas:

_____

_____

_____

_____

_____

Identifying your cause will give meaning and direction to your contributions in life. Consider how some of the great people from history have defined worthy causes:

The purpose of human life is to serve, and to show compassion and the will to help others.

- Albert Schweitzer

What do we live for if it is not to make life less difficult for each other?

- George Eliot

I desire to leave to the men that come after me a remembrance of me in good works.

- Alfred the Great

Be ashamed to die until you have won some victory for humanity.

- Horace Mann

Two Essential Attitudes

Once you have answered the five key questions, you need to adopt two essential attitudes to ensure you remain on the outward-focused path.

Essential Attitude #1: Don't Keep Score

The word "score" is defined as *any account showing indebtedness, an amount recorded as due.* When you give, if you count your contribution as "points" that should be repaid at some later date, then you need to go back to page one of this book and read it all over again.

You need to learn to give without the expectation of getting anything back in return. Do not count how many times you emptied the dishwasher compared to your spouse. Do not count how many months (or years) it's been since your manager praised your work. Do not bake a pie for a friend, drop it off, and then complain because your friend did not call to say thanks. Do not give, wait to see if the other person gives back, and then say, "See, this doesn't work." A scorekeeping attitude will certainly ruin the effectiveness of your outward actions. A scorekeeping attitude will make you miserable.

Give because you know life becomes more—for you and others—when you give. Give because you know every outward action is a good action that defeats evil. Give because you want to make an impact on your world. Give because you know the *Law of Contribution* always works; it's just a matter of time.

We often cannot make the connection between what we give and what we get because we measure the results in the short-term, rather than being able to see the long-term effects of our giving. The principles of the *Law of Contribution* produce consistent results in life when viewed over an appropriate period of time. The long-term effects of outward-focused actions are like a wise financial investment—they pay off big, over a period of time. Outward-focused actions accumulate like the effects of compound interest. Although you might not see the effects on a daily basis, the long-term gains are significant. You rob yourself of life's greatest rewards if you "score keep."

Essential Attitude #2: Provide Others with "Margin"

The actual definition of the word "margin" is the perfect description of the attitude we need to employ when dealing with other people. The word "margin" means *an amount allowed or available beyond what is actually necessary: to allow a margin for error.*

When dealing with other people, we need to give others "margin for error." We need to give them love, respect, kindness, encouragement, care and help "beyond what is actually necessary." We need to do this because generally in life it is all too easy to judge the actions or attitudes of others incorrectly. We interpret others' behaviors—most often incorrectly—because we don't understand their actions or attitudes. We need to stop judging and interpreting others' actions because our judgments prevent us from contributing to them. You cannot care about the needs of others while judging them. By giving others a "margin for error" and level of understanding "beyond what is actually necessary," we give ourselves time and opportunity to understand their real needs. In other words, give people the benefit of the doubt. Do not judge. How might people judge you if they notice you in your worst moments? Would you appreciate some "margin" at those moments? You will enjoy life much more if you are able to provide people in your life with margin.

> *Don't pick on people, jump on their failures, criticize their faults—unless, of course, you want the same treatment. Don't condemn those who are down; that hardness can boomerang. Be easy on people; you'll find life a lot easier. Give away your life; you'll find life given back, but not merely given back—given back with bonus and blessing. Giving, not getting, is the way. Generosity begets generosity.*
>
> - Luke 6:37–38 (The Message)

One FAQ

Perhaps the most commonly asked question when people start trying to live outward-focused lives is, "How do you deal with inward people?" The fact is, once you've read this book and start performing outward actions, you may notice how incredibly inward certain people are. Some people are selfish, self-serving and demonstrate no concern for others at all. Yet you can't get away from them—they work with you, they are family members, they are in-laws or they may even live in the same house as you.

It is difficult to give to people who simply take from you all the time. Yet you want to be outward focused. What do you do?

I have struggled with this question for the four years it took me to write this book. Yet I have continued to be as outward as possible with the hope of learning the answer by experience. My experience has provided me with insight I hope will be of value to you.

First, when I give and do not get back in return, I feel the threat of being taken advantage of. This is a fear-based response I reject. Whenever I find myself saying, "This isn't fair," I remind myself that the purpose of my giving is not to get a "fair" response. The purpose of my giving is to "become" a certain kind of person.

However, over a long period of giving to people, you will notice some people simply take and take and never give in return. It's not that they do not give back to *you* in return, it's that they do not give at *all*—to anyone. Sometimes these people are simply rude, disrespectful and even hurtful. How do you contribute to people like this?

Perhaps a good starting point is to anonymously drop of copy of this book in their mailbox.

In my case, the objective with such people is to always be outward so inward people can "see" an example of outward behavior. Perhaps inward people need to receive outward actions the most. If we do not meet the needs of these people, they have no hope for change. Because I want to be a force for good, I believe I should continue to be outward, even in the most trying circumstances.

Over the past five years, when doing this, I have noticed that some people will take notice and become more outward themselves. I believe people are attracted to worthy values and "right" behavior and will respond if you maintain an outward focus. However, I have also experienced people who did not respond at all after years of intense contribution to their lives. I did not give up. I gave to them for five years but found no change at all in their inward behavior.

As a result, I have adopted the following approach:

> *Rule #1: Never stop being outward because another person is inward toward you.*

Give for a long period of time to set an example.

> *Rule #2: Never become inward because someone else is inward.*

Never ever return a selfish action with a selfish action. If someone is disrespectful, do not let it cause you to be disrespectful. If others around you are selfish, do not become selfish yourself. Let your "worthy cause" guide you.

> *Rule #3: Continue to be outward, but limit your exposure to truly inward people.*

If, after extended outward actions, these people continue to abuse or even hurt you, avoid contact with them. You often will become like those you are around. So you need to ensure you don't become poisoned by spending too much time with inward people. The key here is to limit your exposure to inward, destructive people, but never stop living a life of contribution. Never stop giving; never stop providing others with margin. Give without keeping score. But, when forced to, simply maneuver to avoid being discouraged by inward and destructive forces.

Your approach should always be to promote outward (good) actions. Continue to be outward to help show inward people the way, but you need not purposely allow yourself to be hurt. If you give back to people who give to you, soon enough you will find yourself surrounded by other outward people, and inward people will become less of an issue for you.

The bottom line is this: Use all of your resources to contribute in life in every way that presents itself. Do this, and your life will be filled with abundance, immeasurable joy, fulfillment and satisfaction.

> *Give, and it will be given to you. A good measure, pressed down, shaken together and running over, will be poured into your lap. For with the measure you use, it will be measured to you.*

> - Jesus

Concluding Comments

The *Law of Contribution* is a powerful concept with the power to significantly improve your life and the life of other people in your world. Although the concept is simple, it's not always easy to do, especially because we live in a society that pulls us inward, rather than encouraging us to be outward. If you are going to really benefit from this concept, you need to find a way to remind yourself every single day of the importance of living with an outward focus.

Can I offer you two suggestions to make this happen? First, find people you can share this with. Encourage them to read the book and discuss with them your commitment to a life of contribution. If you can do this with people close to you, they will be able to hold you accountable for staying the course.

Second, I encourage you to complete the form on the following page: My Contribution Commitment. This will serve as a summary of your commitment to a life of contribution and will provide you with a reminder of what you desire to contribute, to whom and why. Complete this form and refer to it often. Your mind requires reminders to keep it focused. This law can significantly impact the quality of your life. Taking time to complete this form and reviewing it daily is a worthwhile investment.

The *Law of Contribution* is more real than you'll know from simply reading this book. If you have the courage to take action and change your outlook, you can begin to experience and understand the real power of this law. I challenge you to make this idea a guiding principle in your life. Although this is the end of this book, I hope it is the beginning of a new outlook for your life.

My Contribution Commitment

I, _____, on this _____ day of
_____, in the year _____, have determined that
from this day forward, I will seek to live a life of contribution.
I am making this decision for the following reason:

_____

_____

_____

I will begin to carry out this commitment in the following ways:

a.)

_____

_____

b.)

_____

_____

c.)

_____

_____

"You get what you want when you give to meet others' needs."

—The *Law of Contribution*

[1] Solomon E. Asch, "Opinions and Social Pressure," *Scientific American*, November 1955, vol. 193, no. 5, 31-35.

[2] Robert B. Cialdini, "Social Proof," *Influence: The Psychology of Persuasion*, (New York: Quill William Morrow, 1984).

[3] Robert B. Cialdini, "Social Proof," *Influence: The Psychology of Persuasion*, (New York: Quill William Morrow, 1984), 133.

[4] PreachingToday.com, Illustrations, "Brad Pitt on The American Dream," excerpt from *Rolling Stone* (10-28-99).

[5] PreachingToday.com, Illustrations, "Empty Success."

[6] PreachingToday.com, Illustrations, "Worshipping God Better Than Super Bowl."

[7] PreachingToday.com, Illustrations, "Quarterback Tom Brady Seeks More," excerpt from Interview with Steve Kroft of *60 Minutes* (11-6-05), www.cbsnews.com

[8] PreachingToday.com, Illustrations, "Halle Barry Says Beauty is Meaningless," excerpt from "Beauty's Beast," www.NewYorkPost.com

[9] http://www.creatingoptimism.com/statistics.html

[10] Study published in *Psychiatric Services*, April 2004. Reported in our health news archive: Pill-Popping Pre-Schoolers, Even Toddlers Get the Blues.

[11] World Health Organization report on mental illness released October 4, 2001. Health news stories: Depression Link to Heart Disease; Hostility, Depression May Boost Heart Disease.

[12] American Foundation for Suicide Prevention, http://www.afsp.org/

[13] American Foundation for Suicide Prevention, http://www.afsp.org/

[14] Arlene Saluter, "Marital Status and Living Arrangements," March 1994, U.S. Bureau of the Census, March 1996, series P20-484, vi.

[15] "The number of divorces annually has almost doubled since 1990, with 264,000 couples formally breaking up in 2000." Reuters, "Japan Cuts Single-Mum Benefits, Blames Divorce Rate," June 7, 9:54 AM, Isabel Reynolds.

[16] "China tries to stem soaring divorce rate," *The Guardian*, March 2, 2005, by Jonathan Watts in Beijing.

[17] Annuaire statistique de la Suisse 1999, Zurich (1999). Cited in Guillod, Olivier, "Switzerland: A New Divorce Law for the New Millennium" in *The International Survey of Family Law*, 2000 Edition. Jordan Publishing Ltd., 2000, 358.

[18] United Press International, March 9, 2005, Ottawa. A growing number of Canadian men are going through divorce more than once, the country's statistical agency, Statistics Canada, reported Wednesday. Using census information, the agency found in 1973 the number of men getting more than one divorce was 5.2 percent. In 2003, that more than tripled to 16.2 percent. The increase among divorced women in the same period was only marginally smaller from 5.4 percent in 1973 to 15.7 percent in 2003.

[19] Department of Health and Human Services, Centers for Disease Control and Prevention. http://www.cdc.gov/nccdphp/dnpa/obesity/index.htm

The two surveys also show that for children aged 2 to 5 years, the prevalence of overweight increased from 5.0 percent to 13.9 percent and for those aged 6 to 11 years prevalence increased from 6.5 percent to 18.8 percent. In teens aged 12 to 19 years prevalence of overweight increased from 5 percent to 17.4 percent.

[20] American Psychological Society survey, 2004.

[21] American Bankruptcy Institute, report, U.S. Bankruptcy Filings 1980-2006 (Business, Non-Business, Total).

[22] Dean Ornish, "The Scientific Basis for the Healing Power of Intimacy," *Love & Survival*, (New York, Harper Perennial, 1999), 42.

[23] Dean Ornish, "The Scientific Basis for the Healing Power of Intimacy," *Love & Survival*, (New York, Harper Perennial, 1999), 44.

[24] PreachingToday.com, Illustrations.

[25] Émile Durkheim, *Suicide: A Study in Sociology*. Trans. John A. Spaulding and George Simpson, (New York: The Free Press, 1951).

[26] Peter F. Drucker, *The Essential Drucker,* (New York: Collins Business, 2001), 20-21.

[27] Martin E.P. Seligman, Ph.D, *Authentic Happiness*, (New York, The Free Press, 2002), 49.

[28] American Foundation for Suicide Prevention, http://www.afsp.org/index.cfm?fuseaction=home.viewpage&page_id=050FE A9F-B064-4092-B1135C3A70DE1FDA

[29] National Library of Australia, "The Diary of William Jon Wills, Friday, 26th [sic] June, 1861," http://www-prod.nla.gov.au/epubs/wills/pages/transcript102.html

[30] John Wooden with Steve Jamison, *My Personal Best: life lessons from an all-American journey*, (New York: McGraw-Hill, 2004).

[31] John Wooden with Steve Jamison, *My Personal Best: life lessons from an all-American journey*, (New York: McGraw-Hill, 2004), 179.

[32] John Wooden with Steve Jamison, *My Personal Best: life lessons from an all-American journey*, (New York: McGraw-Hill, 2004), 115.

[33] John Wooden with Steve Jamison, *My Personal Best: life lessons from an all-American journey*, (New York: McGraw-Hill, 2004), 177.

[34] Jack Welch with Suzy Welch, "Leadership," *Winning*, (New York: Harper-Collins, 2005), 66.

[35] Jack Welch with Suzy Welch, "Voice and Dignity," *Winning*, (New York: HarperCollins, 2005), 53.

[36] Academy of Achievement, George Lucas Interview, Washington, DC, June 19, 1999, http://www.achievement.org/

[37] Academy of Achievement, George Lucas Interview, Washington, DC, June 19, 1999, http://www.achievement.org/

[38] Academy of Achievement, Quincy Jones Interview, London, England, October 28, 2000, http://www.achievement.org/

[39] Tom Peters, *Re-Imagine: Business Excellence in a Disruptive Age*, (New York: DK, 2003).

[40] Academy of Achievement, Sanford Weill Interview, Baltimore, Maryland, May 23, 1997, http://www.achievement.org/

[41] Academy of Achievement, Fredrick W. Smith Interview, Jackson Hole, Wyoming, May 23, 1998, http://www.achievement.org/

[42] Academy of Achievement, Maya Angelou Interview, High Point, North Carolina, January 22, 1997, http://www.achievement.org/

[43] Jack Canfield and Mark Victor Hansen, *Chicken Soup for the Soul, Living Your Dreams,* (Health Communications, Inc., 2003).

[44] PreachingToday.com, Illustrations, "Dexter Manley Had Nothing but Football," originally taken from Jeff Pearlman, "After the Ball," *Psychology Today,* (May/June 2004, 72).

[45] PreachingToday.com, Illustrations, "Dexter Manley Had Nothing but Football," originally taken from Jeff Pearlman, "After the Ball," *Psychology Today,* (May/June 2004, 72).

[46] PreachingToday.com, Illustrations, "*60 Minutes* Producer Looks for Something to Feed His Soul," excerpt from Retired *60 Minutes* Exec Hewitt: 'Where the Hell Do You Go?'" www.DrudgeReportArchives.com (8-20-04).

[47] PreachingToday.com, Illustrations, "David Robinson: More than a Basketball Player," excerpt from *Boston Globe* (5-30-03).

[48] PreachingToday.com, Illustrations, "David Robinson: More than a Basketball Player," excerpt from *Boston Globe* (5-30-03).

[49] PreachingToday.com, Illustrations, "Former Playmate Born to be a Missionary."

[50] Allan Luks with Peggy Payne, "Helpers High: The First Phase," *The Healing Power of Doing Good*, (Lincoln, NE: iUniverse.com, Inc., 1991), 47-49.

[51] Allan Luks with Peggy Payne, "The Calm that Follows: The Second Phase," *The Healing Power of Doing Good*, (Lincoln, NE: iUniverse.com, Inc., 1991), 60.

[52] Allan Luks with Peggy Payne, "Helpers High: The First Phase," *The Healing Power of Doing Good*, (Lincoln, NE: iUniverse.com, Inc., 1991), 48-49.

[53] "The Physiological and Psychological Effects of Compassion and Anger," Research results reported by Glen Rein, Mike Atkinson, and Rollin McCraty in the *Journal of Advancement in Medicine*. 1995; 8(2): 87-105.

[54] Allan Luks with Peggy Payne, "How Our Help Improves," *The Healing Power of Doing Good*, (Lincoln, NE: iUniverse.com, Inc., 1991), 87.

[55] PreachingToday.com, Illustrations, "Volunteering Seniors Live Longer," excerpt from "Senior Volunteers," *Vim & Vigor* magazine.

[56] Diane Swanbrow, "People who give, live longer, ISR study shows," University of Michigan, The University Record Online, November 18, 2002.

[57] Dean Ornish, "The Scientific Basis for the Healing Power of Intimacy," *Love & Survival*, (New York, Harper Perennial, 1999).

[58] Allan Luks with Peggy Payne, "The Calm that Follows: The Second Phase," *The Healing Power of Doing Good*, (Lincoln, NE: iUniverse.com, Inc., 1991), 64.

[59] Carolyn Schwartz, Sc.D., Janice Bell Meisenhelder, DNSc, RN, Yunsheng Ma, MPH and George Reed, Ph.D., article, "Altruistic Social Interest Behaviors Are Associated with Better Mental Health." From the Division of Preventive and Behavioral Medicine, Department of Medicine, University of Massachusetts Medical School, Worcester, Massachusetts (C.S., Y.M., G.R.), and MGH Institute of Health Professions at Massachusetts General Hospital, Charlestown, Massachusetts (J.B.M.).

[60] Allan Luks with Peggy Payne, "How Our Help Improves," *The Healing Power of Doing Good*, (Lincoln, NE: iUniverse.com, Inc., 1991), 101.

[61] Allan Luks with Peggy Payne, "How Our Help Improves," *The Healing Power of Doing Good*, (Lincoln, NE: iUniverse.com, Inc., 1991), 101.

[62] Allan Luks with Peggy Payne, "Introduction," *The Healing Power of Doing Good*, (Lincoln, NE: iUniverse.com, Inc., 1991), 9.

[63] Allan Luks with Peggy Payne, "How Our Help Improves," *The Healing Power of Doing Good*, (Lincoln, NE: iUniverse.com, Inc., 1991), 95.

[64] Dean Ornish, "The Scientific Basis for the Healing Power of Intimacy," *Love & Survival*, (New York, Harper Perennial, 1999), 63.

[65] Dean Ornish, "The Scientific Basis for the Healing Power of Intimacy," *Love & Survival*, (New York, Harper Perennial, 1999), 58.

[66] Dean Ornish, "The Scientific Basis for the Healing Power of Intimacy," *Love & Survival*, (New York, Harper Perennial, 1999), 42.

[67] Dean Ornish, "The Scientific Basis for the Healing Power of Intimacy," *Love & Survival*, (New York, Harper Perennial, 1999), 44.

[68] Dean Ornish, "The Scientific Basis for the Healing Power of Intimacy," *Love & Survival*, (New York, Harper Perennial, 1999), 44.

[69] PreachingToday.com, Illustrations, from "Special Report: Spirituality," *Newsweek* (9-5-05), 48.

[70] PreachingToday.com, Illustrations, "Medical Professionals Believe Spiritual Practices Aid Healing."

[71] Bible. Romans 13:8-10.

[72] Bible. Luke 6:37-38. Version.

[73] Bible. Matt 6:4. Version.

[74] Bible. Proverbs 12:24. Version.

[75] Bible. Proverbs 1:16-19. Version.

[76] Bible. Philippines 2:3. The Message.

[77] PreachingToday.com, Illustrations.

[78] Academy of Achievement, James Cameron Interview, Washington, D.C., June 18, 1999, http://www.achievement.org/

[79] Academy of Achievement, Frederick W. Smith Interview, Jackson Hole, Wyoming, May 23, 1998, http://www.achievement.org/

[80] Academy of Achievement, John Grisham Interview, Williamsburg, Virginia, June 2, 1995, http://www.achievement.org/

[81] PreachingToday.com, Illustrations, "Coach Influenced By Student's E-mail."